PARK SCIENTISTS

GILA MONSTERS, GEYSERS, AND GRIZZLY BEARS IN AMERICA'S OWN BACKYARD

Mary Kay Carson

with photographs by Tom Uhlman

Houghton Mifflin Harcourt
Boston • New York

To our national parks, with deep gratitude for all the glorious sights, wondrous experiences, and lifelong memories they've given us. Happy centennial, National Park Service!

—M.K.C. and T.U.

Photo credits:
Thermal camera images on pages 13 and 16 courtesy of Cheryl Jaworowski, H. P. Heasler, C.M.U. Neale., and Saravanan Sivarajan, "Using Thermal Infrared Imagery and LiDAR in Yellowstone Geyser Basins," Yellowstone Science 18, no. 1. (YEAR), 18–19. Satellite image of Yellowstone on page 15 courtesy of U.S. Geological Survey (USGS). Postcard on page 21 courtesy of National Parks Service (NPS). Grizzly bear collaring and grizzly rebound chart on pages 23 and 24 courtesy of Interagency Grizzly Bear Study Team (IGBST). Saguaro photos on page 45: left unknown, right courtesy of Ray Turner/USGS. Computer-generated maps of salamander ranges and map of salamander DNA samples on pages 54 and 59 courtesy of Amy Luxbacher. Graphics and maps other than those specified above by Yay! Design.

All other photographs by Tom Uhlman.

The book design is by YAY! Design.
The text of this book is set in Century Expanded.
The illustrations are by YAY! Design.

Library of Congress Cataloging-in-Publication Data is on file.
ISBN 978-0-547-79268-2

Manufactured in China
SCP 10 9 8 7 6 5 4 3 2 1
4500449181

ACKNOWLEDGMENTS

We'd like to thank the National Park Service first and foremost for all they do to protect America's most treasured places and share what's special about each park with the public. This book would have been impossible without the aid of countless NPS information officers, rangers, and administrators. We'd especially like to thank the Yellowstone National Park geologists Henry (Hank) Heasler and Cheryl Jaworowski, the Saguaro National Park biologist Don Swann, and Keith Langdon at Great Smoky Mountains National Park.

Scientists are the focus of this book, and we are in their debt for allowing us to tag along, pester them with questions, and take photos. Their willingness to be interviewed and review manuscript drafts was invaluable. Our deepest gratitude goes to the NPS scientists mentioned above, as well as the evolutionary ecologist Amy Luxbacher, the University of Arizona herpetologist Kevin Bonine, Brian Park, firefly researcher extraordinaire Lynn Faust, and Mark Haroldson and Susanna Solieu at the United States Geological Survey Northern Rocky Mountain Science Center.

—Mary Kay Carson and Tom Uhlman

Contents

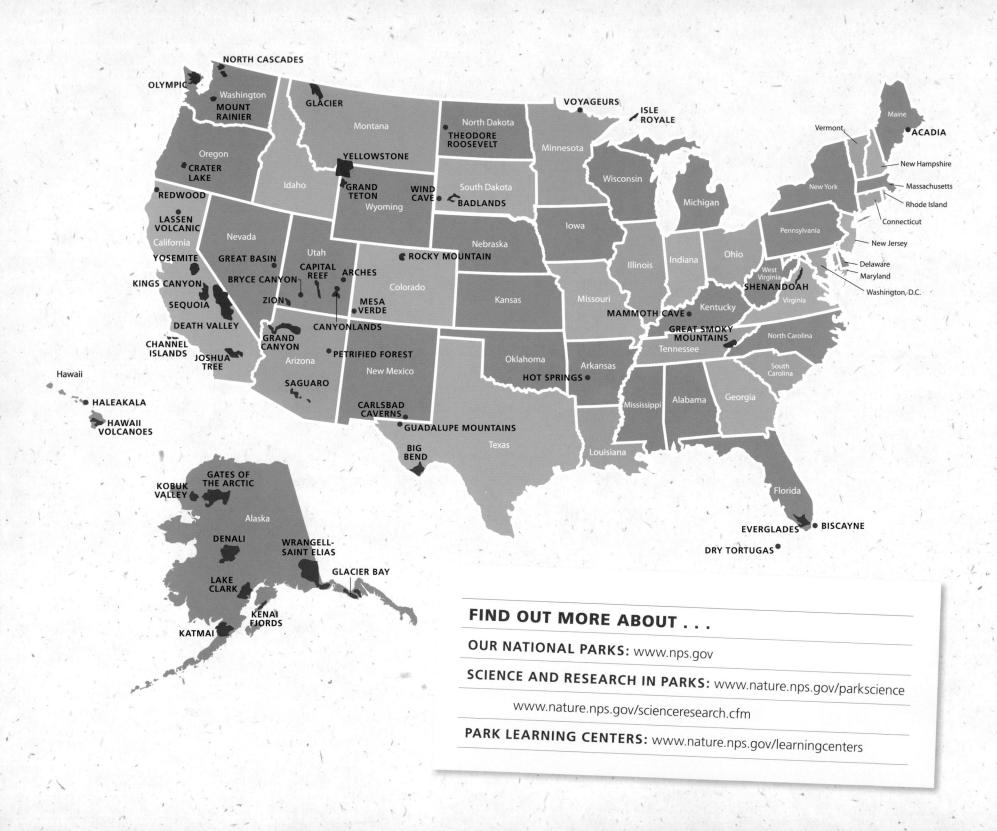

NORTH CASCADES

OLYMPIC

Washington

MOUNT
RAINIER

GLACIER

VOYAGEURS

ISLE
ROYALE

ACADIA

Maine

Vermont

New Hampshire

Oregon

CRATER
LAKE

Montana

Minnesota

Wisconsin

Massachusetts

REDWOOD

Idaho

YELLOWSTONE

North Dakota

THEODORE
ROOSEVELT

Rhode Island

LASSEN
VOLCANIC

GRAND
TETON

WIND
CAVE

South Dakota

BADLANDS

Michigan

New York

Connecticut

New Jersey

California

Nevada

Wyoming

Nebraska

Iowa

Pennsylvania

Delaware

YOSEMITE

GREAT BASIN

Utah

ROCKY MOUNTAIN

Illinois

Indiana

Ohio

Maryland

KINGS CANYON

CAPITAL
REEF

ARCHES

West
Virginia

Washington, D.C.

BRYCE CANYON

SEQUOIA

ZION

Colorado

Kansas

Missouri

Kentucky

SHENANDOAH

Virginia

MESA
VERDE

MAMMOTH CAVE

DEATH VALLEY

CANYONLANDS

GREAT SMOKY
MOUNTAINS

North Carolina

CHANNEL
ISLANDS

GRAND
CANYON

PETRIFIED FOREST

Tennessee

JOSHUA
TREE

Arizona

Oklahoma

Arkansas

South
Carolina

Hawaii

SAGUARO

New Mexico

HOT SPRINGS

Alabama

Georgia

HALEAKALA

CARLSBAD
CAVERNS

Mississippi

HAWAII
VOLCANOES

GUADALUPE MOUNTAINS

Texas

Louisiana

BIG
BEND

GATES OF
THE ARCTIC

Florida

KOBUK
VALLEY

Alaska

EVERGLADES

BISCAYNE

DENALI

WRANGELL-
SAINT ELIAS

DRY TORTUGAS

LAKE
CLARK

GLACIER BAY

KENAI
FJORDS

KATMAI

FIND OUT MORE ABOUT . . .

OUR NATIONAL PARKS: www.nps.gov

SCIENCE AND RESEARCH IN PARKS: www.nature.nps.gov/parkscience

www.nature.nps.gov/scienceresearch.cfm

PARK LEARNING CENTERS: www.nature.nps.gov/learningcenters

America's Natural Laboratories & Living Museums

From Acadia to Zion, America's national parks are the gems of the continent. Each of the fifty-eight national parks is a natural place so treasured and important that it was set aside so future Americans could enjoy it, too.

Taking care of the parks is the responsibility of the National Park Service. NPS depends on scientists to study the best ways to preserve and protect the landscapes and life forms under its care. Park scientists track numbers of bears, eagles, and sequoia trees. They monitor volcanoes, measure glaciers, and look after caves. Scientists in parks collect weather information, restore habitats, and oversee animal populations.

Scientists for Parks and Parks for Scientists

Science is important for managing the natural resources of parks, but parks are also important for science itself. Research goes on in parks that couldn't happen anyplace else.

Because national parks are protected places, researchers are able to do long-term studies of ecosystems, geysers, and climate. Scientists can collect data for years or decades without worrying about a highway going in or a meadow being plowed under. Parks are like natural laboratories.

National parks are also home to plants and animals that live nearly nowhere else—from tiny salamanders in the Great Smoky Mountains to the wolf packs of Yellowstone. If you're a researcher trying to unravel the mysteries of a rare creature or plant, a national park is often the only place to find it. National parks have become living museums.

GREETINGS *from* **YELLOWSTONE** *National Park*

Montana

Idaho

Wyoming

HOW BIG?

3,472 square miles (8,992 km²) of Montana, Wyoming, and Idaho

HOW OLD?

Established in 1872

HOW BUSY?

3–3.5 million visitors per year

REASONS TO GO:

• Largest free-roaming herd of bison in the United States

• 10 gray wolf packs

• First national park in the world

• Active volcano with one of the world's largest calderas

• More than 250 waterfalls

• World's largest collection of geysers, more than 300

FIND OUT MORE ABOUT . . .

PARK: www.nps.gov/yell

YELLOWSTONE SCIENCE:

www.greateryellowstonescience.org

VOLCANO:

volcanoes.usgs.gov/observatories/yvo

GRIZZLIES:

nrmsc.usgs.gov/research/igbst-home.htm

GEYSERS:

www.nps.gov/yell/naturescience/geothermal.htm

Grizz
618

Old Faithful geyser roars to life for two to five minutes about sixteen to seventeen times a day.

Chapter 1

Natural Wonders of Water & Heat

A crowd is gathering near a big half circle of boardwalk lined with benches. People chat in at least a half dozen different languages while little kids play chase and dig through bags of snacks. Soon there is standing room only, and more people keep coming. It's like an audience assembling for a performance, but the stage is a mound of steaming, milky-crusted rock. The backdrop is tall evergreen trees under an impossibly big blue sky. Those waiting for the show keep glancing at watches and phones, and checking cameras.

Grand Prismatic Spring is Yellowstone's largest hot spring, measuring 370 feet (112.8 m) across.

Then things get under way. First there's a rumbling sound, like faraway thunder. Next a fountain of water surges with a growl, sinks with a splash, and then shoots up with a jump, climbing into the sky. It grows to a tower of roaring, pulsing water more than a hundred feet high. Visitors ooh and aah at the fireworks of water. The wind blows spray and mist toward the trees, and billowing clouds of steam soar upward. This is Old Faithful, Yellowstone National Park's famous geyser. Old Faithful erupts every ninety minutes on average—day and night, winter and summer, year after year.

As the geyser shrinks and bubbles to a stop, visitors put away cameras and steer strollers around benches. Some head out on the maze of boardwalks that lead to other geysers nearby. There are thousands in the park, as well as rainbow-colored hot springs, steam vents, and boiling mud pots. "It's why the park is here," says the geologist Hank Heasler. "Yellowstone was founded as the world's first national park because of the hydrothermal [hot water] features." In 1872, a U.S. congressional act set aside land near the headwaters of Yellowstone River to preserve the park's "natural curiosities, or wonders."

Curious Wonders

Hank Heasler is a scientist, a geologist who specializes in geysers and their kin. He's also a uniform-wearing National Park Service ranger, complete with green trousers and a classic ranger hat. There's a reason it looks like an old-style soldier's hat, he says. "Up until 1916 the U.S. Cavalry ran the park," says Hank. In 1916 the National Park Service was created, but it kept some military traditions—like the hat. For now, Hank's hat sits on an empty chair in his office at Yellowstone National

The Yellowstone National Park geologist Hank Heasler.

Park. He and the park's other green-clad geologist, Cheryl Jaworowski, talk about what's on a computer screen in front of them. It's a heat map of the site they're planning to visit today, Norris Geyser Basin. Its hot springs are some of the hottest in the park, with temperatures above boiling. Reports are coming in that some sections are getting hotter.

"In this area here," says Hank, pointing to a stretch of boardwalk on the map, "we started noticing a sickening sweet smell where pine trees are dying." It's time for a quick reconnaissance trip to measure heat and check gases there, says Cheryl. The recon trip won't really be quick, since it's fifty miles (80 km) round trip from park headquarters to Norris Geyser Basin. Yellowstone is a huge park, some 2.2 million acres huge. "We each get 1.1 million acres," they joke. Being a geologist in the park is a big job, but you won't catch them complaining.

Where else can you have an office within the crater of a giant volcano? That's right, Yellowstone National Park sits on top of one of North America's largest volcanoes. "Yellowstone is truly a magical place," says Hank. "And that magic is rooted in the Yellowstone volcano."

A temperature reading of 459°F (237°C), the highest yet in Yellowstone, was recorded just 1,087 feet (326 m) below Norris Geyser Basin.

Old Faithful is just one of 150 geysers within a square mile (2.6 km²) of Yellowstone's Upper Geyser Basin.

Heat Beneath Your Feet

The volcano both created Yellowstone and keeps it going. The current Yellowstone crater, or caldera, is just the latest in a line that the hotspot volcano has created over the past sixteen million years or so. (See "Trail of Eruptions," page 8.) A hotspot is a place where heat from deep inside Earth rises up and melts a region of rock above it. A chamber of underground molten rock, magma, forms above the hotspot. Yellowstone has a lot of heat right beneath your feet: about thirty times as much underground heat as surrounding areas. "That's why we have the world's largest concentration of hydrothermal features," explains Hank.

The giant magma chamber takes care of the "thermal,"

or heat, part of hydrothermal Yellowstone. What about the water, or "hydro," part? Where does Yellowstone's water come from? The volcano gets credit for that, too. Its hotspot has erupted a chain of craters that form a carved-out trough that funnels water-filled mountain rainclouds right to Yellowstone's doorstep. All that rain and melting snow seeps down through layers of crack-riddled rocks. Once the water hits the heat of the magma, it soars to temperatures higher than 400°F (204°C). This superheated water doesn't turn to steam, even though it's hotter than boiling, because of the tremendous pressure created by the weight of rock and water in the fissures above it. Just as hot air is less dense than cool air, hot water is less dense than cool water, so it rises. The superheated water pushes up through cracks and fissures in the rock, the plumbing that feeds the geysers and hot springs.

Whether the rising hot water pools in a hot spring, shoots up as a geyser, turns into a steaming fumarole, or makes a puddle of hot mud depends on the landscape and the chemistry of the rock it travels up through. (See "A Hot Water Wonderland," page 10.) All these different bubbling, spewing, steaming features are related. "Yellowstone's hydrothermal

Cheryl and Hank head out to investigate reports of new hydrothermal activity in Norris Geyser Basin.

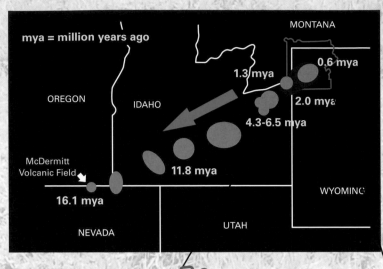

mya = million years ago

MONTANA

0.6 mya

1.3 mya

OREGON IDAHO

2.0 mya

4.3-6.5 mya

11.8 mya

McDermitt
Volcanic Field

WYOMING

16.1 mya

NEVADA UTAH

Trail of Eruptions

Some volcanoes happen where the shifting plates of Earth's crust meet. Others, like the Yellowstone volcano, are created by hotspots under the middle of a crustal plate. As the plate moves (blue arrow), the magma erupts up through new spots, like moving a sheet of paper

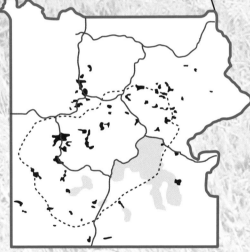

over a lit candle. The Yellowstone hotspot has created a trail of carved-out calderas over millions of years. The track of sunken terrain created by these calderas formed the Snake River Plain, which steers storms and rain right to the park. Parts of Yellowstone get three times the rain and snow as surrounding areas.

The most "recent" eruption created the current caldera in the park, outlined in pink. It's fifty-three by twenty-eight miles (85 by 45 km) wide. That eruption happened 640,000 years ago. Its cataclysmic explosion blasted ash all the way to what is today Iowa, Louisiana, and California.

features are part of a hydrothermal system," explains Cheryl. Each feature is like a bathroom faucet. It's one end result of the house's entire hot-water delivery system, from the electricity that runs the water heater and the cold water that fills it to the pipes and plumbing that get the cold water to the heater and then shuttle the hot water to the sink faucet.

"The National Park Service doesn't just protect the thermal features," says Hank Heasler. "If that were the case, we'd be out there with epoxy and cement making sure Old Faithful wasn't going anywhere." It's the system that's important to protect, like protecting a habitat instead of individual animals. "We're here to protect Yellowstone's natural processes," he says. "So rather than build a permanent boardwalk around a [hot] spring, we'll continually move the boardwalk to keep everyone safe so the spring can move where it wishes." And moving a stretch of boardwalk is just what might have to happen at Norris Geyser Basin, where sections are getting hotter.

Gearing Up

Someone forgot to tell Wyoming that May is springtime. The parking lot at Norris Geyser Basin is blanketed with snow and a harsh wind is turning flurries into stinging darts. Like all good park rangers, Hank and Cheryl are prepared. They layer on coats and insulated pants, hats and thick gloves. Dressing for fieldwork in hydrothermal areas means protection from heat, too, no matter the weather. The geologists wear heat-resistant boots and wool socks. Synthetic socks stick to your skin

Hank checks for dangerous levels of gases near Puff-n-Stuff Geyser.

Riverside Geyser shoots water out at an angle across the Firehole River.

when they melt, explains Cheryl. Ground that's not as solid as it looks is also a hazard. It's often only a brittle crust that easily collapses. That's why there are boardwalks to walk on. "People fall through," says Hank. "Yellowstone has had four times as many deaths from hydrothermal features as [from] grizzly bears."

The science gear comes next. By the time Hank and Cheryl head out, their belts and backpacks are loaded down with temperature guns, an infrared camera, notebooks, regular cameras, temperature probes, a psychrometer, and gas detectors. An odd box-shaped device hangs around Hank's neck, too. Little lights on it keep flashing. "It will warn us if gas levels become dangerous," he says. Good to know.

Gases are certainly all around us. The whole basin has a slight odor of sulfurous rotten eggs, or as one young visitor along the trail commented, "It smells like farts." Odd odors aside, Norris Geyser Basin is a wonderland. The view from the overlook is otherworldly. There are plumes of steam coming from countless gurgling geysers and hot spring pools the colors of pistachio and turquoise. Winding among it all are little green- and rust-colored channels of water filled with odd algae and heat-loving microbes. The scene is so surreal that it feels like watching video from another planet, or going back in time to a newly born Earth. Only the distant evergreen trees look familiar. Even the boardwalk paths look peculiar from the overlook. Some paths connect or loop around, while others suddenly dead end with DANGER! signs.

Heading Out

The boardwalk trail that Hank and Cheryl are walking along is

A Hot Water Wonderland

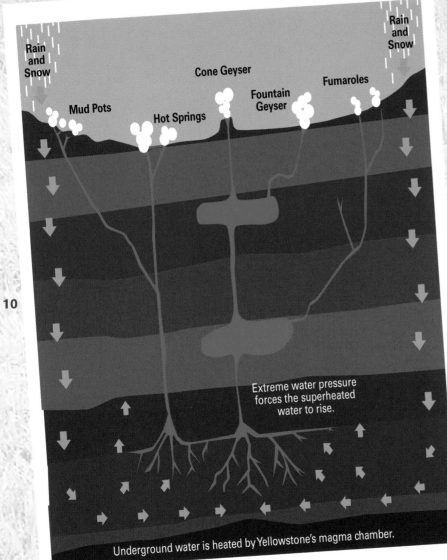

Rain
and
Snow

Rain
and
Snow

Cone Geyser

Fountain
Geyser

Fumaroles

Mud Pots

Hot Springs

Extreme water pressure forces the superheated water to rise.

Underground water is heated by Yellowstone's magma chamber.

Rain and melting snow seep into the ground where the Yellowstone volcano's magma chamber heats the water, sending it rising up to the surface to create these different kinds of hydrothermal features.

Punch Bowl Spring is a hot spring 12 feet (3.7 m) across in Yellowstone's Upper Geyser Basin.

Hot springs are pools of heated water. Temperatures can range from warm to boiling, and the water's color also varies depending on the minerals and microbes in it. Most of the hot springs at Yellowstone are fed by water rich in silica from rhyolite rock. Deposited silica sculpts the wavy, scalloped edges of these pools. The exception is Mammoth Hot Springs, which is fed by water that rises instead through limestone. The calcite in this water is the same mineral that creates cave formations, and Mammoth Hot Springs has amazing limestone terraces.

Fumaroles, or steam vents, are hot springs in which the water has completely turned to steam and other gases by the time it reaches the surface.

Hank and Cheryl watch the plumes billowing from Black Growler Steam Vent.

Geysers are hot springs whose water can't freely flow onto the surface because the flow is constricted in its underground pathways through rock. Boiling water collects in underground reservoirs. As this superheated water rises, it quickly boils into steam and also creates expanding bubbles that rise, blocking the narrowing pathway. Once enough pressure has built up behind the bubble blockage, it pushes up the layer of water all at once, like uncapping a bottle. The geyser comes to life, splashing or surging with water. This pressure release starts a chain reaction of violent boiling and steam explosions as superheated water below shoots upward through the vent—an eruption. Because water bursts out faster than the geyser's reservoir can refill with heated water, the eruption eventually slows as the water cools. **Cone geysers** erupt in a tall shooting jet of water from a built-up cone-shaped opening of deposited silica called geyserite. **Fountain geysers** shoot water in different directions and from a larger opening that fills with water, like a pool.

Old Faithful can eject water to heights of 184 feet (56 m).

Mud pots are pools of scalding-hot mud at the top of a steam vent. The mud is created by microbes that ooze out rock-dissolving acid as they consume sulfur gas for energy. The mud bubbles as gases escape through the hot, wet clay.

Mud pots, like this one at Yellowstone's Mud Volcano area, bubble mud and burp out smelly gases.

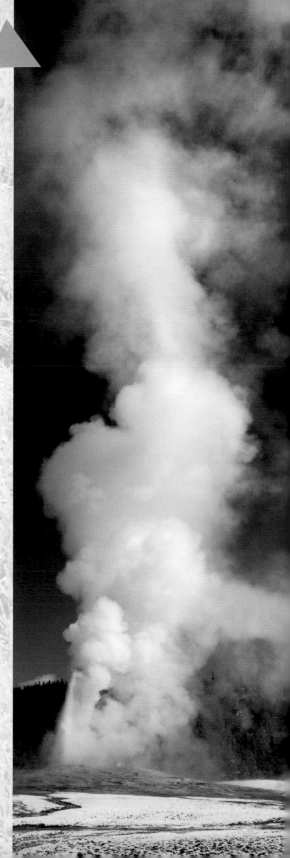

Hank Heasler pushes a temperature probe into the crusty ground near a warm section of boardwalk in Norris Geyser Basin (above). **Hank then uses an infrared camera** (below) **to record images of heat.**

covered in trampled snow, except for the spot where the geologists stop and set their gear down. "You can see that this section of boardwalk is dry and clear of snow," says Cheryl. Then she points out the nearby dead and dying trees. The ground around them is covered not in snow, but with something yellow and crusty. Both are signs of new hydrothermal activity. The ground is getting hotter here. This is the site they've come to check out.

Hank crawls under a hand railing and cautiously lowers himself off the boardwalk. Boots on the ground, he pulls a long pole out of his backpack. It's a probe that measures temperature all along its length. Hank pushes it down into the soft, warm ground and waits. "Ninety-two point three degrees Celsius [198°F]," Hank calls out. Cheryl writes it down in a field log, saying, "That's about boiling point at this elevation." When Hank pulls the probe out, sure enough, a pencil-thick plume of steam follows. It's a mini fumarole, or steam vent. He stomps on the spot a few times to close it off. Are gases besides steamy water vapor coming out too? Hank points to the yellowish ground near the dead trees, explaining that the bright-colored crust is sulfate salts, left behind by escaping steam loaded with sulfur. "This is a very good indicator that this is not an area you want to be walking around in," says Hank. His beeping gas detector confirms it. Hank reads his instruments, rattling off the gas amounts to Cheryl for sulfur dioxide, hydrogen sulfide, and carbon dioxide. Some of the levels would be lethal in a closed space. The cold whipping wind is now our welcome friend.

Seeing Heat

On the boardwalk above Hank, Cheryl aims what looks like a video camera toward the spot he's measuring. "It's a thermal imaging, or infrared, camera," she explains. It takes a snapshot of heat by recording infrared (IR) light, instead of visible light like a regular camera. (See IR image on this page.) The image will be used to compare the site with past and future thermal pictures to track changes. "We want to carefully monitor this," says Hank about the recon site. "Things are changing rapidly." They'll recommend closing off the section of boardwalk if it becomes unsafe for visitors. Nearby boardwalks were rerouted a few years ago because of high thermal readings. It'll happen again. Change is what Yellowstone is all about. "Especially geologically," says Hank. Most geologists talk about changes over hundreds of thousands to millions of years. "Here in Yellowstone we get to see changes daily, which is quite a treat for geologists."

It's one of the many things Hank Heasler likes about working in America's oldest national park. Yellowstone has been part of his life since he was a kid growing up about eighty miles (129 km) away. "My parents began bringing me here when I was six years old," he says. The memory of seeing blue pools and exploding geysers as a boy has stayed with him. "I remember thinking even then: How do all these work?" Now he gets to help answer that question with scientists and also share his knowledge with the public.

Helping to keep visitors safe is just one part of the job Yellowstone's geologists do. "The hydrothermal system that we are trying to protect here is globally rare," says Hank. The volcano provides heat, the rain and snow replenish the underground water, and the chemistry of minerals in the rocks plays a part, too. Plus the crucial plumbing system of rock fractures and fissures is created by the region's plentiful earthquakes (thousands every year). All of these factors combine to create the world's biggest concentration of geysers and other hydrothermal features—more than ten thousand in total.

Monitoring an individual hydrothermal feature isn't

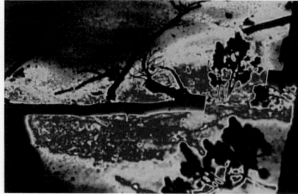

These images show the same section of warming ground just below the boardwalk at Norris Basin. **The regular photograph** *(top)* **is a visible light image. The infrared image** *(above)* **shows heat seeping up through the ground.**

13

14

Cheryl uses a temperature gun to measure the water temperature of a hot spring in Norris Geyser Basin.

the same thing as understanding the entire hydrothermal system that created it, however. "If Old Faithful changes, what does that say about the hydrothermal system?" asks Hank. "One of the challenges here is, how do you monitor hydrothermal systems?" This is the big picture that Hank and Cheryl are trying to understand. The Yellowstone geologists gather information from satellite images, data collected with helicopters and airplanes, and numbers from on-the-ground temperature loggers, water-flow measurements, and chemical analyses of water in the hydrothermal system. "Each one uses a different scale, gives you a different perspective, and gets you different information," explains Hank.

Cheryl Jaworowski is the remote-sensing expert. "I decided I wanted to be a geologist in my first semester of my first geology class," she says with a big smile. The infrared camera Cheryl was using earlier is also mounted on an aircraft to record nighttime thermal images of large areas. Cheryl then takes the maps of heat levels the IR camera creates and fits them to daytime aerial pictures and GPS maps. (See IR map on page 16.) Maps of the same places taken over time allow the geologists to track changes in cooling and heating.

Knowing What's Normal

The thermal IR maps and pictures are one way geologists are trying to figure out what exactly is normal for Yellowstone's hydrothermal areas. How can you tell if you're sick if you don't know what your normal

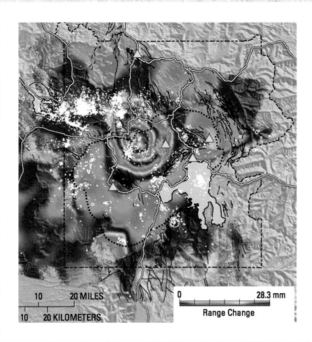

This satellite image of the Yellowstone volcano shows ground deformation. The areas of biggest change are in red and yellow.

A Virtual Volcano Observatory

If the Yellowstone volcano that creates the parks' hydrothermal system erupted, the entire continent would be affected. "The risk of an eruption has about the same odds as a one-mile asteroid hitting Earth," says the Yellowstone geologist Hank Heasler. Not very likely, in other words, but both would be quite catastrophic. Experts keep close tabs on the giant volcano, continually checking in on it. "We have a very good volcano monitoring system in Yellowstone and will know if the volcano, and when the volcano, starts to become excited," says Hank.

The United States Geological Survey (USGS) heads up the Yellowstone Volcano Observatory. It's a virtual observatory, not a building or place, but rather a group of people from Yellowstone National Park and the University of Utah who work with the USGS to monitor the volcano. There are three indicators they look to that signal a possible eruption on the way. "The first is increased earthquakes in one particular area," says Hank. Yellowstone has thousands of small earthquakes a year. The only area in the United States with more earthquake activity is San Andreas, California. Not only are there fault lines going through Yellowstone, but the caldera floor itself moves. It rises and falls inches per year over different areas, like the chest of a giant slowly breathing.

A large increase in this rising and falling, called ground deformation, is the second indicator of a coming eruption. The third sign is big changes in hydrothermal activity: "geyser basins becoming hotter and producing more gas," explains Hank. Since none of these signs of a stirring volcano is happening, you don't need to worry. "Yellowstone is a great place to come and visit and experience the beauty of the volcano directly," says Hank.

15

blood pressure, temperature, and heart rate are? The vital signs for Yellowstone's hydrothermal system are heat, water, and chemistry—how much heat is coming out; and how much water is seeping in and where it's coming from, how much and where the hot water is flowing; and the chemical makeup of the minerals. "We're trying to get those variables nailed down," explains Hank. "Then when there are significant changes, we can with some certainty say the cause of them—whether they are natural or human-caused." Once what is normal is known for each hydrothermal site, the geologists can better monitor and protect the hydrothermal system for future visitors.

"That's our focus right now," agrees Cheryl. She says they've already got six years of good thermal map data for a few hydrothermal areas, including Old Faithful. The information tells the geologists how much heat variation is natural—and normal. Old Faithful should be able to amaze the three million annual visitors to Yellowstone National Park for years to come. Seeing the gigantic geyser leap up into the blue sky is not a sight to miss.

Geyser Hill

Old Faithful

Myriad Group

	40°-70° C
	30°-40° C
	20°-30° C
	15°-20° C
	10°-15° C
	5°-10° C

0   100   200   300   400

This infrared map shows the ground temperatures around a number of Yellowstone's thermal areas, including Old Faithful.

The geologists Cheryl and Hank monitor temperatures and gas levels along a trail in Norris Geyser Basin.

Chapter 2

Yellowstone's Biggest Bears

A grizzly bear searches for an early spring meal in Yellowstone National Park.

Stay in your vehicles!" a voice booms. At the other end of the loudspeaker is Dave Page, a park ranger at Yellowstone National Park. His park SUV is blocking off a roadside pullout, its roof lights flashing blue and red. The small parking area looks out over a river valley covered in snow-dusted spring grass. Out in that field is a very large animal—a bear. It's a grizzly bear, to be exact, rotund and brown like milk chocolate, with humpy shoulders and round ears. Its head is near the ground, huge nostrils taking in the scents stirred up in overturned dirt. The bear lumbers around swiping gently at the grass, sending clods flying with its massive finger-length claws.

These tourists are dangerously—and illegally—close to a grizzly bear crossing a road in Yellowstone National Park. Visitors can be fined for being less than 100 yards away.

A line of minivans, cars, and RVs begins to form as curious tourists slow down for a look. "Keep moving!" the ranger commands, waving cars along. "This bear is getting too comfortable being close to the road." Proving the ranger's point, the bear seems unaware of all the fuss and continues searching for food. Ranger Dave says that the bear has been hanging around the parking area a lot lately. Roads are dangerous places for bears. Not only do cars hit them, but roads put bears in contact with people—rarely a good thing. People can get hurt, and bears often end up being killed for safety reasons. "It's not safe for people or for bears," says Dave.

Yelling and clapping haven't fazed this bear. "So the next step is to fire cracker rounds to scare the bear off," Dave explains. The green-uniformed ranger strides to the edge of the

parking area, takes a wide stance, and raises a shotgun to his shoulder. It's loaded with loud firecrackers packed inside shell cartridges. Dave aims and fires. POP! The shell sails toward the bear and explodes with a smoky boom. The grizzly looks up just as a second round goes off and, without a glance back, lopes across the field, heading for a line of distant trees.

The Bear Scientist

Spring is when bears come out of hibernation—with a powerful appetite. The roadside bear the ranger ran off will now go forage elsewhere for food. "Our grizzly bears in Yellowstone are in a hole in the ground for four to six months out of the year," says Mark Haroldson. He's a wildlife biologist who does bear research in Yellowstone. Bears that live in the Northern Rockies survive the long winter by hibernating. During those months, the bears' breathing slows and their hearts beat half as fast. The bears don't eat or drink, surviving instead off the stored fat they put on in autumn. They don't even urinate or poop. The bodies of hibernating bears somehow recycle the waste and use the proteins to make muscle. Medical scientists are studying the secrets of bear hibernation, says Mark. What they discover could someday help bedridden and ill humans.

Even more amazing is that mother grizzlies are pregnant and give birth while hibernating. The cubs are born tiny, blind, and helpless in the dead of winter. The cubs manage to nurse and sleep with their hibernating mother, growing rapidly. By the time spring comes, they're big enough to leave the den with Mom in search of food.

"Bears are fascinating," says Mark Haroldson with a sparkle in his eye. "I've spent my whole life working with bears." He's studied wild bears in Minnesota, New Mexico,

Mark Haroldson, wildlife biologist and bear scientist, with one of the collars his team uses to track bears in Yellowstone.

This photo from 1970 shows how grizzlies used to feed regularly in dumps.

Colorado, Wyoming, and Montana. As a wildlife biologist, Mark studies wild animal populations and their habitats. He's researched grizzly bears in and around Yellowstone for the Interagency Grizzly Bear Study Team (known as the Study Team) for the past thirty years. "The Study Team was formed out of the controversy around the dump closures in the late sixties, early seventies," Mark explains. Up until the 1960s, bears were allowed—even encouraged—to rummage through dumps and garbage pits in the park. Generations of Yellowstone's bears grew up eating hotel kitchen scraps and campers' leftovers. And generations of tourists fed bears from cars and gathered to "bear watch" at garbage pits. So why close

off dumps to grizzlies? To understand the story of Yellowstone's grizzly bears, it helps to look at the very beginnings of the park itself.

Wild Entertainment

Geysers and hot springs got Yellowstone National Park created. The millions of acres of wilderness set aside along with the hydrothermal features weren't so special in 1872. Back then the American West seemed endless. Bison herds of millions thundered across vast lands prowled by mountain lions and wolves. Unbelievably, within a few decades much of that wilderness and wildlife would be gone—plowed under and built

Where Grizzlies Roam

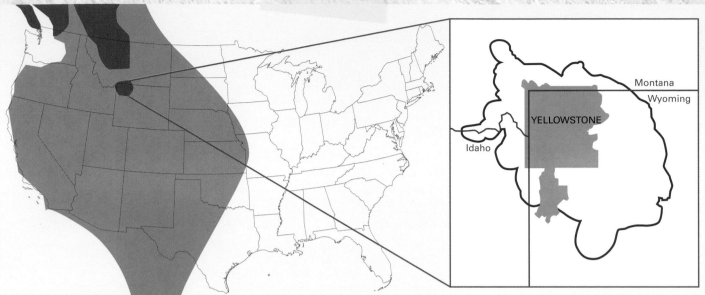

The tan shaded area of the United States *(left)* is the historic range of grizzly bears. The dark brown areas are where grizzly bears remain today, including Yellowstone. The park (in pink) is part of the Greater Yellowstone Ecosystem. The dark blue line outlines the area where grizzlies live within the region.

Montana

Wyoming

YELLOWSTONE

Idaho

over by farms and towns, taken over by roads, ranches, and railroads. Yellowstone ended up a last refuge for many wild animals, especially those needing lots of room to roam, like huge herds of bison and big predators. It became the anchor of the largest intact ecosystem of its kind left on the continent. Today, it's the only place in North America where all the continent's major predators can be found together: cougars, grizzly and black bears, badgers, coyotes, wolves, wolverines, and lynx.

Without the park's protection, it's doubtful that all these predators would still live in the region. That includes grizzly bears, who today remain in only 2 percent of their entire historic range in the lower forty-eight states. (See map above.)

"I think the park probably had a lot to do with maintaining security for the bears in Yellowstone," says Mark.

Creating Yellowstone in 1872 protected habitats and wildlife, but the popular park's many visitors created less-than-wild bears. Over time, the garbage-gobbling bears became a famous attraction. They were one of the sights that everyone came to see at Yellowstone, like Old Faithful.

After decades of troublesome run-ins between bears and visitors, the park decided to close all the garbage dumps. Too many people were getting hurt by "problem" bears that ended up killed for safety reasons. With human scraps cut off, conflict between hungry grizzlies and campers, ranchers, and hunters in and around Yellowstone increased—and so did bear deaths. Between 1967 and 1972, at least 229 grizzlies within the Yellowstone ecosystem died. There was a lot of arguing about closing the dumps, visitor safety, and starving bears. Was the grizzly bear population in serious trouble? "There was a lot of uncertainty as to the status and trend of numbers of bears," explains Mark. The Interagency Grizzly Bear Study Team started up in 1973 to figure out exactly what was going on with grizzlies, says Mark, and grizzly bears were listed as a threatened species by the federal government under the Endangered Species Act two years later. He's been part of the Study Team for three decades now and works at the Northern Rocky Mountain Science Center in Bozeman, Montana.

Grizzly GPS

At the Science Center, Mark Haroldson sits at a table that's covered in bear collars. They are wide and made of faux leather, looking like collars for extremely big dogs. Square electronic components are glued on to them. Mark holds up a collar with alarmingly large teeth marks in it. "This one was in the den with the bear all winter long," he says, assessing the damage. "I think he played with it as a chew toy." Grizzly bears aren't easy study subjects. Being big, dangerous, long-clawed, and sharp-toothed is partly why. Grizzlies also get around. Females have average home ranges of about 120 square miles (310 km²), and males roam within an average area of about 312 square miles (810 km²), with some males covering triple that. That's an enormous expanse anywhere, but much of Yellowstone is difficult to get to. The backcountry preferred by bears can be many miles from any road. And the park is only a fraction of the Study Team's research area.

The Study Team tracks bears in the Greater Yellowstone Ecosystem (GYE), not just Yellowstone National Park's. The GYE is six to seven times larger than the park itself. It spans an area the size of West Virginia, and about 19,000 square miles (50,000 km²) of that is grizzly territory. (See map on page 20.) Collars make tracking grizzly bears possible. "We live capture and handle on average eighty to ninety different bears a year, and radio-collar most of the captured bears that are big enough to wear them," says Mark. The Study Team uses two kinds: telemetry collars and global positioning system (GPS) collars. The telemetry collars send out signals that scientists on the

This postcard from the 1910s shows a favorite pastime of early visitors to Yellowstone.

ground or flying over in aircraft pick up with receivers.

"These are GPS collars," says Mark, picking up a different-looking collar. "These are collecting data and storing it on here, and we get a location every hundred minutes or so." The collar does this day and night from April through December, turning itself off during winter hibernation. The

Mark Haroldson works on bear collars at the Northern Rocky Mountain Science Center in Bozeman, Montana.

Grizzly #618

The mother of this newly born bison calf protects it from a gray wolf.

GPS collars have electronic clocks on them that are set with a day and time to unlock. After a couple of years around a grizzly bear's neck, the collar beeps, springs pop it open, and it falls off. "We can use telemetry to find the collar, pick it up, and bring it into the office," says Mark. We'll hook it up to our computer and download our data. We'll get a good track of where that bear spent its life the previous two years."

Collaring bears is part of how the Study Team counts grizzlies. Information gathered from the collared bears gives the Study Team information on the age of first-time mothers, how many cubs they have and how often, and causes of death. "We use that data to develop survival rates," says Mark Haroldson. What percentages of collared bears survive over the years goes into the equations that estimate the population trend for grizzlies in the region. These math equations model the population's trend— whether the number of grizzly bears is increasing, declining, or staying the same.

Even after grizzly bears were listed as a threatened species in 1975, their numbers kept dropping. Stricter garbage disposal rules in the early 1980s on forest service lands and campgrounds outside of the park helped finally turn it around, says Mark. How are Yellowstone's grizzly bears doing today? "The population is stable to slightly increasing," says Mark. Around six hundred grizzly bears now live in the Greater Yellowstone Ecosystem.

Changing with the Times

Grizzly bears are once again living wild in Yellowstone, no longer begging for leftovers or entertaining tourists at dumps. People and their decisions still greatly affect the large bears, however. Over 80 percent of all documented grizzly bear deaths in Yellowstone are human-caused. Dozens of grizzlies die each year in clashes with people. Some are trapped and removed from homes where they've been attracted to food and garbage, or for killing cattle and sheep. Others are killed by elk or deer hunters in self-defense, and a few are hit by cars or trucks. People have also changed the bears' ecosystem and continue to alter it. Some changes were made on purpose. Wolves were reintroduced to Yellowstone in 1995. Wolves may compete with bears for prey, but they also create food for grizzlies. Adult grizzly bears will take an elk kill away from wolves. Whether wolves in the ecosystem are a win or a loss for grizzly bears isn't clear yet, but they have changed the balance.

Wolves are native to Yellowstone. Other introduced species are not, including game fish. Spawning cutthroat trout were once an important grizzly bear food. That's changed since nonnative game fish pushed out the cutthroat trout. Introduced fish like lake trout live longer, breed more, eat cutthroats, and live in waters too deep for bears to fish. Since cutthroat trout disappeared from the shallow waters around Yellowstone Lake, the bears no longer have fish to eat. Grizzly bears eat an amazing variety of different foods throughout the year (see

top left: **Grizzly researchers bait and capture bears in large culvert traps. The bear is tranquillized before researchers open the hatch.**

middle left: **Researchers work quickly to gather data on a sedated grizzly bear. They measure its length and its head and neck size, and collect hair and blood samples.**

bottom left: **Mark Haroldson fits a sedated grizzly bear with a radio collar.**

above: **The map on the computer screen shows grizzly bear locations identified by collars.**

A Grizzly Rebound

Legend:
- GYE population estimate
- Cubs of the year
- Females with cubs

Population estimate: 100, 200, 300, 400, 500, 600

Cub and female counts: 20, 40, 60, 80, 100, 120

1987 2010

Early spring snowstorms make meals difficult for grizzlies to find in Yellowstone National Park.

chart on page 26). A grizzly bear eats any living or dead animal, from bison to ants, as well as feasting on dandelions, mushrooms, grasses, and seeds. "Bears are opportunistic omnivores," says Mark. That means they eat pretty much anything they can find. Bears learn easily and teach one another. "Bears are really smart," explains Mark. "There's a lot of culture learning among them." A mother bear that raises her cubs near Yellowstone Lake teaches them to fish, for example. Cubs growing up far from Yellowstone Lake never learn to fish. "Those moms are teaching those cubs a different way to make a living."

Keeping track of what Yellowstone's grizzly bears are eating is a big part of what the Study Team does. "We want to know what habitats they're using and what they're utilizing in those habitats," says Mark. In early spring Study Team scientists hike, ski, or snowshoe into the backcountry to collect data on carcasses of elk, bison, deer, and other animals. These half-frozen leftovers are important food for hungry bears coming out of their long hibernation. Study Team scientists collect information on what bears eat, as well as bear signs—tracks and trails, scat and fur, claw and rubbing marks, and whatever else the bears leave behind. The seeds of the whitebark pine are another important grizzly bear food that the Study Team tracks. The oily seeds are full of fatty calories and help grizzly bears pack on the pounds before heading into hibernation. Unfortunately many of Yellowstone's whitebark pines are dying.

A Changing Diet and Future

A journey up to Yellowstone National Park's higher elevations makes it obvious. Along the foot of alpine peaks is an evergreen carpet full of brown patches—dead whitebark pines. One killer is the mountain pine beetle, a native whose tree-chomping larvae

Grizzly bear cubs stay with their mother for two to three years.

A Month-by-Month Grizzly Menu

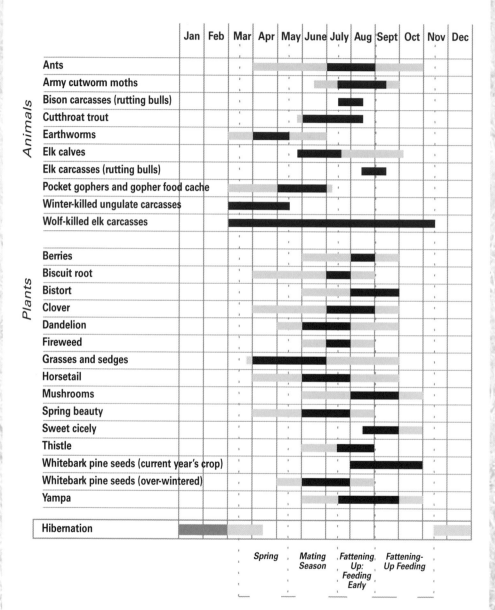

	Jan	Feb	Mar	Apr	May	June	July	Aug	Sept	Oct	Nov	Dec
Animals												
Ants												
Army cutworm moths												
Bison carcasses (rutting bulls)												
Cutthroat trout												
Earthworms												
Elk calves												
Elk carcasses (rutting bulls)												
Pocket gophers and gopher food cache												
Winter-killed ungulate carcasses												
Wolf-killed elk carcasses												
Plants												
Berries												
Biscuit root												
Bistort												
Clover												
Dandelion												
Fireweed												
Grasses and sedges												
Horsetail												
Mushrooms												
Spring beauty												
Sweet cicely												
Thistle												
Whitebark pine seeds (current year's crop)												
Whitebark pine seeds (over-wintered)												
Yampa												
Hibernation												

Spring   Mating Season   Fattening Up: Feeding Early   Fattening-Up Feeding

The average male grizzly bear is about seven feet (2 m) tall and weighs four hundred to six hundred pounds (180–270 kg).

kill the trees. Their populations have exploded in recent years, thanks to milder winters that many blame on global climate change. An introduced fungus, called white pine blister rust, is harming the trees too. These pest problems mean fewer nut-producing pinecones for bears. What's going on with whitebark pines is why grizzlies remain protected and listed under the Endangered Species Act even though their population has recovered.

In some areas where grizzlies used to eat lots of pine nuts, bears are now feeding on other foods, including mushrooms, Mark says. Where bears once caught Yellowstone cutthroat trout, they are preying more on elk calves. Bears can survive on different foods, as long as they get enough to eat overall. "The question will be, if we continue to lose calories available to bears from whitebark pine, can they find calories in other places that will make up for the loss?" asks Mark. The Study Team is keeping an eye on it. "Every bear we catch, we try to determine its condition, its percent fat," explains Mark. By tracking the amount of fat on female bears over time and matching it with who is successfully having cubs, they'll know whether grizzlies are making up the lost pine nut calories.

The greater concern is perhaps how, and where, grizzlies will go looking for food. Searching outside of the park brings bears into conflict with hunters, roads, and livestock, and brings other kinds of trouble. "Everywhere they go outside of public land there is the urban, human interface," says Mark Haroldson. "It is a minefield for them." Nearly four decades of collaring bears has made one thing clear to the Study Team: grizzlies do best where people are few and far between. However, humans are still linked to the long-term survival of grizzlies in Yellowstone. Climate change, introduced plants, fish and pests, as well as the building of towns and roads, make a difference to grizzly bears. Grizzly bears are more than a symbol of Yellowstone's wilderness; they depend on it for survival.

Grizzly bear tracks are distinctive, with toes in a straight line.

27

GREETINGS *from* SAGUARO *National Park*

Arizona

HOW BIG?

143 square miles (370 km²) of Arizona

HOW OLD?

Established in 1933

HOW BUSY?

750,000 visitors per year

REASONS TO GO:

- Six species of rattlesnake
- 25 species of cactus
- 18 species of hummingbirds
- 150 miles (241 km) of hiking trails
- Colorful sunsets
- Huge stands of North America's largest cactus, the saguaro

FIND OUT MORE ABOUT . . .

PARK: www.nps.gov/sagu

SONORAN DESERT SCIENCE:

www.desertmuseum.org/center

SOUTHWEST SCIENCE:

www.southwestlearning.org

SAGUARO CACTI:

www.nps.gov/sagu/naturescience/saguaro_q_a.htm

GILA MONSTERS:

tiny.cc/GilaMonster [www.eebweb.arizona.edu/faculty/

bonine/Welcome.html]

BIOBLITZ:

www.nationalgeographic.com/explorers/projects/bioblitz

Chapter 3
Tracking Monsters

Researchers use radio telemetry to track Gila monsters in and around Saguaro National Park.

Saguaro National Park, in southern Arizona, looks like a giant cactus garden. Acres of evenly spaced cacti in every imaginable spiny, prickly shape grow out of pastel-colored gravel. The park's Sonoran Desert home is full of fierce plants adapted to living thirsty. Tough grasses, waxy-leafed bushes, and smooth-skinned trees fill the space between cacti with smells of cooking herbs, tar, and soap. Sounds are part of the desert, too. The background buzz of insects is broken by a hawk's call—and there's also a *beep . . . beep . . . beep* noise.

The beeping is coming from a small black box carried by a man wearing a wide-brimmed hat. Brian Park also holds up what looks like an old-fashioned TV antenna. The beeping box and antenna are radio telemetry instruments. Brian is using them to zero in on a critter with a radio transmitter inside of it. The beeps are getting louder. That means she's nearby, Brian tells the half dozen people hiking up a hill with him. Being careful to avoid the prickly pear and fishhook cacti, he sets down his gear near a hump of granite. The sun-hatted hikers circle the big rock and begin inspecting its crevices and cracks.

"She's visible, everybody!" Brian announces. He's stooped over and is using a small mirror to bounce strong desert sunlight underneath the rock. Everyone moves in for a look. "I can see her head in there," someone says. A crouching middle-aged woman puts a hand on the rock to steady herself. "I wouldn't put your fingers there," warns Brian. Why not? The animal stuffed underneath the rock can deliver a painful, venomous bite. It's a Gila (HEE-la) monster.

Monstrous Lizards

Gila monsters are big lizards with powerful, clamping, venomous jaws. (See "WARNING! Armed and Armored," page 32.) They're the largest lizards in the United States, growing up to two feet (61 cm) long and weighing up to three pounds (1.4 kg). "Gila monsters belong to a reptile group called Monstersauria," says Kevin Bonine. He's a scientist at the University of Arizona and heads up a Gila monster study. Monstersaurs roamed alongside *T. rexes* and other dinosaurs

The researcher Brian Park and volunteer citizen scientists zero in on a Gila monster using radio telemetry.

The Gila monster's name comes from the Gila River region of Arizona.

a hundred million years ago. Today, the only other remaining "monster lizard" species is the beaded lizard, who is also big and venemous.

Gila monsters make their homes in the deserts of the southwestern United States and northern Mexico. They're common in Arizona, and it's hard to mistake the large, slow-moving lizards. Gila monsters are chunky, low-to-the-ground lizards covered in pink, orange, and black skin studded with tiny pebbly bumps. "Gila monsters are an iconic species of the Sonoran Desert," says Kevin. But being famous hasn't gotten Gila monsters much scientific attention over the years. Gila monsters aren't easy to study. They're nocturnal much of the

year and spend a lot of their time in underground burrows. Gila monsters don't need to be out constantly searching for food, like a bird or mouse does. A large adult lizard may eat only a few times a year. "Their favorite food is a nest full of baby bunnies or quail eggs," says Kevin. Gila monsters are expert nest raiders.

Kevin Bonine is a herpetologist, a scientist who studies amphibians and reptiles. He's hoping his research will solve some Gila monster mysteries. "We're not sure how many Gila monsters are out there, or exactly what they do all year," says Kevin. Scientists don't even know the time of year the lizards are born. Gila monster moms lay eggs in underground

Gila monsters look ready for a fight. Their skin is covered in round bumps filled with bone, called osteoderms. This studded skin covers their head, tail, and body like armor. Long, powerful claws for digging and strong, powerful clamping jaws are their weapons—and so is their venom.

"They have venom glands in their lower jaw," explains Brian Park, a Gila monster researcher. Unlike a rattlesnake, a Gila monster can't inject venom. The venom simply mixes into its saliva, or spit, when they feel threatened. "When they bite you, they latch on," explains Brian, "and all that venom trickles into you." Sharp, grooved teeth help deliver it, as does chewing on the victim for a good long time. A Gila monster bite is intensely painful, but not fatal to humans. There's no antivenom treatment, and the bite can make a person sick for weeks. Medical scientists are interested in the venom that Gila monsters make. They've copied unique chemicals found in the lizard's saliva and are testing them as possible drugs for diabetes, attention deficit disorder, and memory loss.

While Gila monsters look tough, they aren't aggressive and don't go after people. If you see one, it's likely to be shuffling away from you. "If you don't ever stick a finger in front of one or pick it up, you should never have a problem," says Brian. "Most bites happen when harassing a Gila monster." If pain and suffering aren't reason enough to steer clear of Gila monsters, how about the law? As a protected species, harassing, handling, collecting, or killing them is illegal. Gila monsters were the first protected reptile in Arizona and in 1952 became the first protected venomous animal in the United States.

**WARNING!
Armed and
Armored**

Gila monsters have strong forelimbs and claws for digging burrows and raiding nests. Their scientific name is *Heloderma suspectum*.

burrows in the late summer, and baby Gila hatchlings leave burrows the following spring. When exactly they hatch during those eight to ten months is their well-kept secret. Perhaps they hatch in autumn and the hatchlings spend the winter underground. "Or are they in the egg for a heck of a long time?" asks Kevin. The list of needed answers about Gila monsters in and around Saguaro National Park is long, says Kevin. How far do they travel in a year? Do they leave the park? How many burrows do they use? Do roads and housing developments affect them? "There's a whole lot of mystery," Kevin says.

Female #291

The Gila monster that Brian Park has tracked down is providing some clues. Gila monster #291 has a radio inside her. Kevin's team has implanted tiny transmitters inside

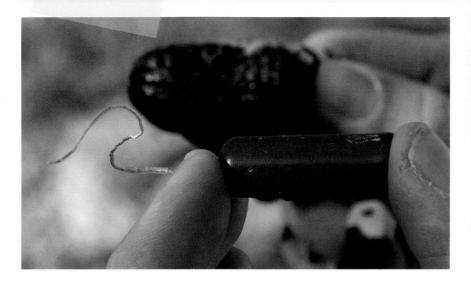

The radio transmitters like this one that scientists surgically implant into Gila monsters are about the size of an AA battery. A radio collar wouldn't work because it would get in a Gila monster's way as it squeezed under rocks or into holes.

eight different Gilas. Now that Brian's telemetry receiver has found #291 under the big granite rock, Brian and his helpers get to work.

As she snoozes undisturbed in her burrow, they write down the lizard's GPS position, note the time of day, take air temperature and humidity measurements, and list the kinds of plants growing around her rock. All of this information will help scientists figure out how much Gila monsters travel about—and why. The study is finding that how much a Gila gets around depends on its age, sex, habitat, and the season. During spring and early summer, for example, when males are out looking for mates they will wander more than females generally. Female #291 may be on the move, too. She was down the hill in the picnic area near the road just two weeks

The herpetologist Kevin Bonine uses radio telemetry to track the wanderings of Gila monsters.

ago, says Brian. Is #291 looking for a place to spend the winter?

Gila monsters don't have permanent homes. An abandoned packrat burrow might be a good cool summer spot, while squeezing under a sunny rock can provide a cozy winter shelter. As with all reptiles, the body temperature of Gila monsters changes with their environment. The beeping radio inside the tracked Gila monster also estimates its body temperature. The warmer the body temperature, the faster the radio beeps. Researchers carefully record the body temperature of each lizard every time they track it. That way they know how much warmer or cooler the animal is in the various shelters it uses throughout the year. The rock that #291 is currently under gets a lot of sun on one side, says Brian. It might make a decent winter home.

BioBlitz and Microchips

Filling out #291's data sheet is taking a bit longer than usual. Everyone except Brian Park is new to Gila monster science. The hikers are volunteers taking part in BioBlitz, a twenty-four-hour scientific inventory of every species in Saguaro National Park (see "Survey Says!," p. 48) are among the thousands of citizen scientists helping out during the event. So that lots of people can join in the activities and learn about biodiversity, BioBlitzes often take place in national parks near urban areas like Saguaro National Park. The city of Tucson, Arizona, fills the space between the park's two separate halves.

Brian Park and BioBlitz volunteers collect information about Gila monster #291 in Saguaro National Park.

"Citizen science is important for involving the community," says Kevin. It's a big part of the study that researchers at the University of Arizona, including Kevin Bonine and Brian Park, are doing in Saguaro. In fact, their Gila Monster Project depends on it. "We try to get the public to send us their sightings," explains Kevin. How? They've posted colorful signs at kiosks near trails and in visitor centers. The signs say HAVE YOU SEEN ME? above a plump pink Gila monster. Below the photo are instructions for documenting the sighting and sending in the information. Kevin says, "People out hiking

and park staff can really help us out." The key is taking a photograph of the Gila monster that clearly shows its markings. "The pattern on each individual is like a fingerprint," says Kevin. Researchers use the color patterns to identify individual Gila monsters.

Sometimes the researchers receive a photo from a citizen scientist that matches a Gila monster they've tagged, "which is pretty exciting," says Kevin. The Gila Monster Project has been tagging the large lizards with microchips since 2009. Each tiny microchip tag looks like a metal grain of rice. It's the same kind

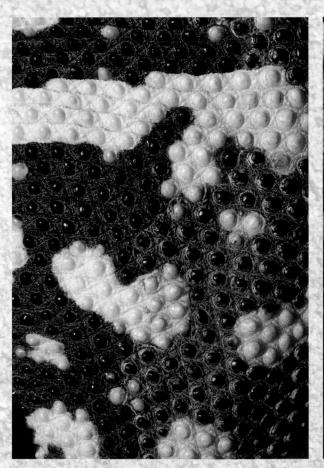

The skin bumps of Gila monsters have tiny bones in them called osteoderms *(close-up far left)*. The patterns of color are unique to each animal, as shown at left. This Gila monster tag *(above)* is a small metal pellet with an ID microchip in it.

By implanting a radio transmitter inside a Gila monster, researchers can track the lizard's movements over time with radio telemetry.

of ID microchip tag that veterinarians use for dogs, cats, and other pets. Each tag has an identification number that a handheld scanner can read. "We've tagged more than one hundred and fifty Gila monsters," says Kevin. Every new Gila monster that the field biologists come across gets a tag.

Catching Monsters

The punishing desert sun is sinking toward the distant mountaintops, but it's still 85°F (29°C). The giant piled-up pink and beige boulders soak up heat like pizza stones. Kevin doesn't seem to break a sweat, however, even though he's got one hand firmly gripping a Gila monster. In his other hand is what looks

above: **The white plastic probe collects mouth cells full of DNA when chewed on.**

right: **Kevin estimates how much fat is stored in this Gila monster's tail by measuring the volume of water it displaces when pushed into the graduated cylinder. Well-fed, healthy Gila monsters have fat tails.**

like a small plastic toothbrush. Kevin puts the softer end of the plastic tool on the lizard's closed mouth—and gives it a nudge. How do you get a Gila monster to open wide? "You talk very nicely to him," jokes Kevin. Evidently it's true. The smoky-pink lizard takes the bait, giving the plastic prod a few chomps. It will leave behind enough mouth cells for a DNA sample.

Researchers measure each animal's head width using calipers.

Body length is measured, as well as overall length from snout to tail tip.

Gila Monster Project researchers such as Kevin and Brian hike and drive in Saguaro National Park regularly, tracking and checking in on the Gila monsters with radios and looking for new ones. When they come across a Gila monster, they catch it—very carefully. Foot-and-a-half-long medical tongs can help hold a squirmy one still. Each animal is measured, weighed,

photographed, and injected with a microchip tag under the skin. Researchers also measure the volume of its fat-filled tail to find out how well fed it is. The plastic stick chewed on by the lizard is sent off to a DNA lab for analysis. "It gives us the ability to answer a whole range of questions," says Kevin—big-picture questions such as how similar Saguaro's Gila monsters are

to those in California or Mexico, and how closely related the lizards in the park are to one another.

One of the goals of the Gila Monster Project is learning what these large, venomous lizards need to thrive, so they can be protected in the future. Are highways and fences separating Gila monsters and creating small, fragmented populations? DNA studies can tell if they are losing genetic diversity or inbreeding. Are new neighborhoods taking away needed habitat? Comparing the lives of Gila monsters not in the park with those inside it can help find out. "We want to learn a lot more about them both in the protected areas of the park as well as in the wildland-urban interface," says Kevin. "That's where they interact with roads and cars, people and dogs, and that sort of thing."

The Sonoran Desert is something special—fragile and harsh, dazzling and mysterious. "My life has always been tied to the desert," says Kevin of the Sonoran and its creatures. He hopes that the work of the Gila Monster Project will ensure that future generations have that connection, too. "We are hoping to get data that will be useful for decades to come," he says, "so we can learn a lot more about these magnificent lizards and help to protect them as well." If you're lucky enough to see a Gila monster in Saguaro National Park, take its picture and write down where you saw it. But keep your fingers to yourself.

Gila monsters live in the Mojave, Sonoran, and Chihuahuan Deserts of North America. They smell by picking up scent particles with their purplish forked tongues (top left). **Gila monsters have feet and claws made for digging burrows and uncovering prey nests** (bottom left).

Chapter 4

Saguaros
are the
largest
cacti in
the United
States.

Counting Cacti

Saguaros are giants of the cactus world. They are tree-trunk thick and rise up high into the desert sky. How tall are saguaros, exactly? That's what a group of teenagers are spending their Saturday trying to figure out. The students are armed with measuring sticks, pencils, clipboards—and fake eyeglasses.

Alex Varela is wearing a pair under the brim of a green ball cap. Tied to the nose bridge of the lenseless eyeglasses is a red string. The string's other end is attached to the center of a wooden meter stick that Alex holds at arm's length. "How tall is this saguaro?" fellow student Arron Davis asks. Alex raises and lowers the meter stick while looking toward the spiky green pillar of cactus. "Three-point-three meters [10.8 ft]," says Alex. Arron fills in a data sheet, saying, "Okay, got it, three-point-three." That's higher than a ten-foot basketball rim, but not that tall for a saguaro. An older saguaro can be four times that height.

"How many arms? Any holes?" asks Arron. The students count and write down the medium-size saguaro's branches and its nest holes. On cue, a Gila woodpecker streaks by and settles into a neighboring saguaro's nest hole. "So cool!" says fellow student Almomese Ramirez, looking up from her clipboard. These Tucson, Arizona, high school students are among the thousands of citizen scientists who took part in the twenty-four-hour species survey at Saguaro National Park called BioBlitz. (See "Survey Says!," page 48.) The information collected by the teens will be added to a saguaro cactus census databank that goes back generations. Hundreds of saguaro surveyors have studied the giant cacti in the park's Section 17 over the past seventy years.

Park's Prickly Namesake

"Saguaro National Park was established in 1933," says Don Swann, a park biologist. The park was created to protect a cactus forest of large saguaros in the Rincon Mountains outside of Tucson, Arizona. What's the big deal with these beloved desert plants? Don thinks there are a couple of reasons why visitors come from all over the world to look at their famous saguaros. Seeing the green giants covering entire desert hillsides is an impressive sight. "And saguaros are unusual-looking," says Don. "They look somewhat like people." Many saguaro parts have humanlike names. Branches are

below left: **Alex Varela, a citizen scientist and high school student, wears glasses tied to a 50-centimeter (20-in) red string that attaches to a meter stick. The string ensures that distance between his eye and the meter stick is exactly 50 centimeters.**

below right: **Tucson high school students measure out five meters from the base of the saguaro. This is where the person holding the meter stick must stand.**

A saguaro cactus that's as tall as a four-story building and weighs seven tons started life as a tiny, round black seed as many as two hundred years ago.

1 inch = 5–7 years: Seedlings are vulnerable to heavy rain, burning sun, hungry critters, and trampling feet the first ten years.

1 foot = 15–20 years: A young saguaro survives under the shade and protection of a nurse tree.

6–8 feet = 35–40 years: Saguaros start making flowers at about this age. Bats, birds, and bugs drink their nectar and help pollinate the large, white waxy blossoms.

15 feet = 75 years: Once at this height, a saguaro will start sprouting arm buds. Woodpeckers drill holes in saguaros for nests that are later used as homes by wrens, owls, snakes, and mice.

Up to 50 feet = 150–200 years: The sweet red fruit produced by mature saguaros is eaten by coyotes, foxes, javelina, rodents, birds, and people, too.

43

The biologist Don Swann first fell in love with deserts visiting Australia. "I remember thinking, *Wow, we have deserts like this in the U.S. I should check it out,*" he says.

called *arms*, old nests are *boots*, and the woody leftovers of a dead saguaro *skeleton* are called *ribs*.

What else is so special about saguaros? "They live longer than we do," says Don. "Some of the saguaros here have probably been around for two hundred years." That means they were here when Arizona belonged to Mexico and slavery was still legal. Back then it was mostly foot traffic that passed by the saguaros, but today jetliners stream overhead. "Saguaros give us a long-term perspective," says Don. They're a perfect example of what the national parks are for, he says. "By protecting these resources, people will be able to come out fifty or a hundred years from now and enjoy saguaros." But the secure future of the park's saguaros

Citizen scientists measure saguaro cacti during BioBlitz at Saguaro National Park.

1935

Today

The saguaro forest today *(right)* **has yet to recover to what it was in 1935** *(left)*.

wasn't always so certain. There was a time when their survival chances seemed slim.

Section 17 Census

Soon after the park's creation some eighty years ago, many of its largest saguaros were dying. Why? Saguaro National Park turned to science to find out. In 1941 the saguaros in a square-mile section of the park, called Section 17, became part of an experiment. "They measured and marked every single saguaro in Section 17, about 13,000 saguaros," explains Don Swann. At the time, researchers thought a disease was killing the large cacti. So they removed the sickly-looking saguaros from one area and tracked those left behind. The condition and growth of those saguaros over time were compared with cacti in plots where seemingly ill saguaros were left alongside healthy ones. "After ten years there wasn't any difference between the saguaros in and outside the control areas," says Don. "It wasn't a contagious disease." So why were large saguaros still dying?

"Science doesn't always give you the answers right away," says Don. "Science can be messy." It can take a long time to tease out the truth. "It's hard to do experiments with a plant that lives two hundred years." The Section 17 study soldiered on, collecting data year after year. In fact, counting and measuring the saguaros of Section 17 never stopped. It's one of the longest-running annual monitoring programs for any species in the U.S. national parks. Every year, plots within the square-mile area are surveyed by scientists with help from citizen scientist volunteers. The 2011 BioBlitz was the first time

below: **Tucson high school students measure saguaro cacti during BioBlitz at Saguaro National Park.**

right: **Citizen science volunteers count arms and nest holes of an ancient saguaro.**

right: **BioBlitz volunteers use a measuring stick to get the height of smaller saguaro cacti.**

the entire Section 17 was resurveyed just like seventy years before. The findings from seven decades of study are welcome news. The saguaros are coming back. There aren't as many as there were in 1941 yet, but today there are lots of young saguaros.

Did scientists ever figure out what happened to all those older saguaros? "What we think killed most of those saguaros around 1940 was a couple of really cold freeze events," says Don. Saguaros are mostly water, and long freezes burst their tissues, the way a can of soda explodes in the freezer. Severe cold snaps, not disease, killed the large saguaros. "But the bigger problem was that there were no young ones to replace them," explains Don. Small seedling saguaros are fragile and depend on so-called nurse trees to protect them. Mesquite, acacia, and palo verde trees shelter young saguaros from heat and sun, wind and frost. Many nurse trees were cut for lumber and firewood before the park came into being. Cattle also grazed in the cactus forest, trampling newborn saguaros. Tree cutting and cattle grazing likely destroyed a generation of saguaros, but no one knows for certain. "Saguaros grow so slowly, you don't fully understand what is going on with the population until decades after the changes," explains Don.

It is certain that the park's protection helped save the saguaros. Cattle grazing and logging of nurse trees stopped in the 1930s. Once the protective trees came back, a new generation of young saguaros survived. "All the things we did to protect the saguaros seem to have worked," says Don Swann. Back at Section 17, the work goes on. The Tucson

47

An Old Forest Grows Young

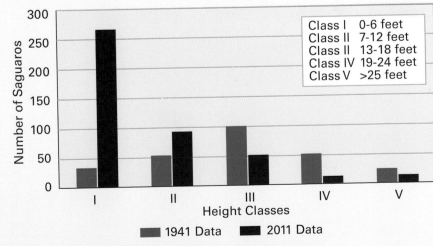

Class I	0-6 feet
Class II	7-12 feet
Class II	13-18 feet
Class IV	19-24 feet
Class V	>25 feet

Most of the saguaros in Section 17 today are young and still small.

teenagers take a break to drink water and pull spines out of their jeans. It's already 90°F (32°C), but no one suggests quitting. Like the generations of citizen scientist Section 17 surveyors before them, the high-schoolers take the study seriously. The saguaros are important to them, too. Nothing could make Don Swann happier. Saguaro National Park's future depends on young people becoming real, true stewards of this park, says Don. "Hopefully these kids will end up being caring citizens—people who really care about the park and want to protect it."

Survey Says!

Every year during the decade leading up to the one hundredth anniversary of the National Park Service in 2016, a different national park holds a BioBlitz hosted by the National Geographic Society. BioBlitz is a twenty-four-hour scientific inventory of all the species in a park.

The 2011 BioBlitz at Saguaro National Park was a great success. More than five thousand scientists, citizen scientists, volunteers, and students searched for species, learned about the Sonoran Desert, and celebrated the diversity of life on earth. They identified more than 1,200 kinds of plants, insects, animals, and fungi. Many of the species had never been identified in the park before. One microscopic creature called a water bear, or tardigrade, had never been seen in the state of Arizona before. Motion-activated cameras set up in the backcountry also captured photos of some secretive and seldom-seen desert mammals like mountain lion cubs and coati, which are house cat-size raccoon cousins.

left: **Saguaro branches, or arms, grow upward. A severe freeze sometimes damages branches, causing them to droop, but the growing tip always turns back upward.**

bottom left: **Scientists kept a running tally of species identified during BioBlitz at Saguaro National Park.**

bottom right: **Each saguaro flower is two to three inches (5–7 cm) across. The blooms open at night and close the following afternoon.**

bioblitz
A 24-HOUR SPECIES INVENTORY
tally

			1
Amphibians		8 6	4
Birds			
Fungus		4 1	1
Invertebrates	1		
Mammals		2	1
Non- Vascular Plants			0
Reptiles		2	2
Vascular Plants	3	0	7

Total Species Count 5 8 2

GREETINGS from GREAT SMOKY MOUNTAINS
National Park

Tennessee

North Carolina

HOW BIG?

800 square miles (2,072 km²) of Tennessee and North Carolina

HOW OLD? Established in 1934

HOW BUSY? 9 million visitors per year

REASONS TO GO:

• 10,000+ species, more than any other area of equal size

  in a temperate climate

• A United Nations International Biosphere Reserve

• 100 backcountry campsites

• Observation tower atop Clingmans Dome, the highest point

  in Tennessee at more than 6,640 feet (2 km)

• Herd of more than 130 elk

• 1,500 black bears

FIND OUT MORE ABOUT . . .

PARK: www.nps.gov/grsm

SMOKIES SCIENCE:

www.nps.gov/grsm/naturescience/pk-homepage.htm

SALAMANDERS:

www.nps.gov/grsm/naturescience/amphibians.htm

FIREFLIES:

www.firefly.org

BIOLUMINESCENCE:

science.howstuffworks.com/zoology/all-about-animals/

bioluminescence3.htm

Chapter 5
Smoky Mountains Salamanders

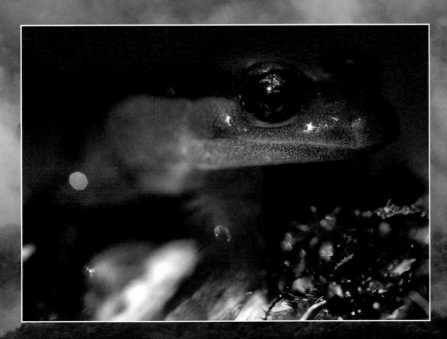

It's high noon, but it seems like dusk in the shadowy, dim forest. Only small patches of gray sky poke through the foggy treetops. Drizzling raindrops fall from twisted branches onto fir boughs as they tumble down and soak into a carpet of dewy moss, slippery leaf litter, and slimy logs. The whole world here looks hazy green, smells musty, and feels wet.

Amy Luxbacher doesn't mind the damp. She kneels down near a chunk of spongy bark the size of a shelf and pushes back the hood of her rain jacket. Amy lifts the bark with her left hand and with a swift, smooth scoop of her right, comes up a winner. "Here's one," she says, opening her cupped hand. On her palm is an adorable four-legged creature. It has huge, round black eyes, teeny little toes, and a mouth with a bit of an overbite.

Red-cheeked salamanders are gray to bluish black with orange- to red-colored patches on the sides of their heads. They range from three and a half to seven inches (9–18 cm) in length from snout to tail tip.

The evolutionary ecologist Amy Luxbacher searches for salamanders under a soggy log in Great Smoky Mountains National Park.

Adding to its cartoonlike cuteness are its namesake red patches of skin on each side of its shiny gray head. This is the red-cheeked salamander.

"Such a cute face," says Amy with a smile. Amy Luxbacher is a scientist who studies salamanders, so maybe she's biased, but she is interested in more than just their good looks. "The red-cheeked salamander is a pretty special animal," says Amy. "It doesn't occur anywhere else in the world except in this national park." Its only home is the Appalachian highlands in Great Smoky Mountains National Park.

Salamander Central

This is where some of the highest peaks of the ancient tumbledown Appalachian Mountains can be found. No other area of equal size outside the tropics has as many different species of plants and animals. More than thirty different species of salamanders earn the Smoky Mountains the title of Salamander Capital of the World. They range from pygmy salamanders the size of a paperclip to cat-size aquatic hellbenders. Salamanders are a big part of the mountain ecosystem. They eat more prey for their weight than any other animal in the park—including bears!

Salamanders are amphibians, like frogs and toads. Salamanders and newts (a kind of salamander) are sometimes confused with lizards, but the two are very different. Lizards are reptiles and have scales and claws, and they lay leathery-shelled eggs on land. Frogs, salamanders, and other amphibians are covered in moist skin, lay their jellylike eggs in wet or watery places, and undergo metamorphosis. Just like frogs start out as tadpoles, salamanders also have a larval stage. This need for water and wetness is why so many salamanders make

The Blue Ridge two-lined salamander has two black stripes down the side of its yellow-orange body.

As its name hints, the pygmy salamander is tiny. The smallest salamander in the Smokies reaches lengths of only one and a half to two inches (3.7–5.1 cm).

The Southern Appalachian salamander is slimy and oozes gluey mucus as a defense.

their home in the wispy mists of the Smoky Mountains. "All that moisture in the air that gives these mountains their name also makes this area ideal for salamanders to live," says Amy.

Life on Land

Many salamanders stay moist by simply living in or near water. But there are some, including the red-cheeked salamander, that live their entire lives on land. Instead of finding a pond to breed in, red-cheeked salamander mothers lay their eggs in soggy soil under bark or logs. A newborn salamander develops from egg to larva to adult all within the watery world of its egg, hatching out as a miniature adult.

"Being a terrestrial salamander has some benefits," says Amy. A full-time life on land means more kinds of prey, from ants and spiders to snails and centipedes. But living away from water can have a deadly downside—suffocating. Red-cheeked

salamanders breathe through their wet skin. They have no lungs. To survive, these salamanders must live in places damp enough to keep their skin moist and breathing. "That only includes certain areas in Great Smoky Mountains National Park that are above three thousand feet (914 m) in elevation and where the temperatures remain cool and the humidity remains high," explains Amy.

It's all about staying within a budget, or what scientists like Amy call an energy budget. Food adds energy, but finding food uses energy. Food must be worth the effort to find it for an animal to survive. For a salamander, the big tradeoff is water. Moisture starts evaporating from its skin the second it departs its damp home. The longer a salamander must be out looking for food in the open air, exposed to wind and warmth, the more water it loses. "They have to live where they can afford to dig and forage without losing too much moisture," explains Amy.

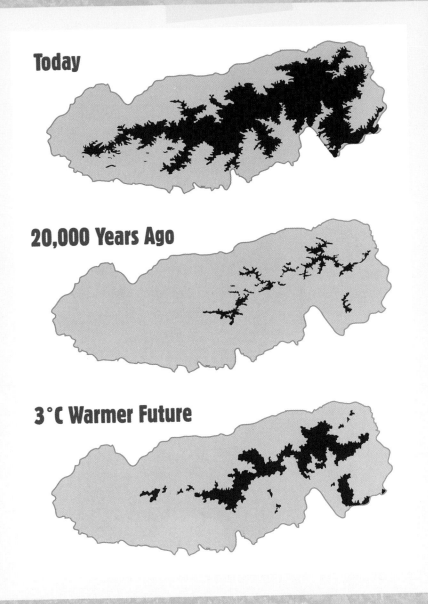

Today

20,000 Years Ago

3°C Warmer Future

The computer-generated map on the top shows the current areas in Great Smoky Mountains National Park that are cool and wet enough for red-cheeked salamanders to stay within their energy budget (in red). The map in the middle shows where those same microclimate conditions likely occurred 20,000 years ago. The lower map shows where suitable areas of red-cheeked salamander microclimate will likely be after a 5–6°F (3°C) rise in global temperature.

Making a living in the warmer, drier forest farther down the mountain would blow their energy budget. It would cost the salamanders too much in lost water to feed themselves.

"The red-cheeked salamander has a very narrow range of conditions in which it can successfully live and reproduce," says Amy. Only about 575 square miles (1,489 km²) of the park has a cool and humid enough climate at a high enough elevation—a suitable microclimate—for them. Scientists know exactly where these salamander sweet-spots are in the park. They've mapped them with the help of powerful computer models. Measurements of temperature and humidity near the ground, wind speeds, and topography are fed into the model. The computer crunches and combines the data to create a map predicting where red-cheeked salamanders can live within their energy budget. (See "Today" map at left.) The map has been tested, too. The areas of salamander-suitable microclimate on the map match up with where red-cheeked salamanders live—at least for now.

A Warming World

"My research is on how climate change may affect the red-cheeked salamander," says Amy Luxbacher. Earth's overall temperature is rising due to polluting greenhouse gases. As the planet warms, climates across the globe are changing. Scientists predict that the hotter and drier lowlands of the Smokies will likely expand up the mountains and replace the current cool, moist microclimate. "For species like the red-cheeked salamander that already live at the tops of the mountains," explains Amy, "the risk is that the narrow range of climate conditions in which it can live may disappear entirely—leaving these salamanders literally high and dry at the tops of the mountains."

Will mountain salamanders survive in a warmer world? One 2010 study of future climate predictions said that the red-cheeked salamander will likely be extinct by the year 2050. Is that really going to happen? Amy says it's hard to know. Her research is looking to the past for clues about the future. She is studying what happened to the salamanders when the climate changed thousands of years ago. What she finds could help predict the fate of the species in a warmer future.

Using the Past to Predict the Future

Amy Luxbacher is an evolutionary ecologist. The ecologist part means she studies how and why salamanders live where they do today. The evolutionary part is about understanding how they evolved to be there. Like much of North America, the Smokies cooled and warmed many times during glacial cycles lasting tens of thousands of years. About twenty thousand years ago the climate in the Smokies was about 14–22°F (8-12°C) colder than today. "These mountains weren't covered in glaciers," explains Amy. But it was colder—too cold for salamanders in some places. When she and her colleagues put the climate conditions of twenty thousand years ago into the model, it makes a map predicting where the microclimates good for red-cheeked salamanders would have been (see "20,000 Years Ago" map on p. 54). According to the model, the mountaintops would have been too cold, but areas lower down the mountains would have met their needs. "I found there were basically three pockets of suitable habitat where the species could have survived," explains Amy.

A map that shows pockets of suitable microclimate is interesting, but how can you know if red-cheeked salamanders actually lived there twenty thousand years ago? Fossils would

Amy gets a closer look at a salamander in Great Smoky Mountains National Park.

provide proof. "Unfortunately salamanders don't fossilize very well," says Amy. Where else can scientists look for the history of a species' evolution? Inside something that's been passed down from generation to generation for millions of years—genes.

The DNA in genes is more than a genetic instruction manual for making a living thing. It's also a history book, with clues about ancestry. You probably know of people who've had their DNA tested to find out whom they're related to or where their family came from. This is what Amy is doing too.

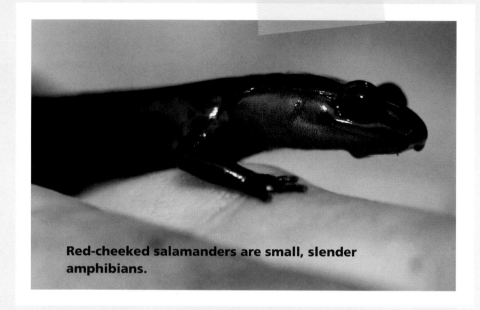
Red-cheeked salamanders are small, slender amphibians.

How? She's testing the DNA of red-cheeked salamanders from different sections of the park. By looking at their genetic differences she'll be able to map where closely related salamanders likely lived during the past colder climate. "From that information we can reconstruct the story about how populations have changed over time from past to present," explains Amy. "And then we can apply that to the future."

Tails of Science

Amy rolls over a big, soft, rotting log. She's back on the salamander hunt in the cool, misty Smoky Mountains highland forest. Before you can study salamander DNA, you have to catch a lot of salamanders. Something dark and shiny disappears into the dirt below. "The soil is so soft underneath from all that decaying stuff that they can burrow quickly," says Amy. "It's gone." She carefully moves the log back over the cinnamon-colored soil. There will be others. Amy has had lots of practice catching small, slippery creatures.

"I've always really liked reptiles and amphibians, since I was a little girl," she says. Spending time on her grandparents' farm turned out to be job training. "I would be out in the woods looking for salamanders or by the pond trying to catch frogs." Amy followed her interest in animals to college, where she studied zoology and considered becoming a veterinarian. She decided that wasn't for her. "I like seeing animals in their natural environment, and I like to be outside," she explains. "I like hiking—and getting dirty!" Amy got her wish there. Her knees are covered in mud and soggy leaves as she crouches near some fallen branches. She peeks under a thick sheet of bark, does a quick grab, and comes up with a handful of dirt and a salamander. Amy holds it gently, her thumb and forefinger around its middle so its tail hangs free.

The DNA is collected from the tail tip. "You just apply a little bit of pressure and it comes right off," says Amy. She uses tweezers to pinch off the very tip of the red-cheeked salamander's tail. The minute quarter-inch (0.6 cm) bit of tail looks like a splinter or thorn in between the metal tweezer's ends. A moving splinter. "This one's not super wiggly," says Amy, putting the tiny gray tip into a plastic vial. "Sometimes they wiggle more." Salamanders grow their tails back, so it doesn't hurt the animal, and there's no blood. Lizards and salamanders can drop their tails on purpose to escape a predator, who can be confused by an abandoned squirming tail. "It's called caudal autotomy," explains Amy as she labels the vial. Next she opens a field notebook and writes down the tail-snipped salamander's sex, size, and cheek color brightness, and the coordinates from her handheld GPS. "Off you go," says Amy as she puts the slippery test subject back under the log where she found it.

Amy Luxbacher drops a wiggly salamander tail tip into a collection vial *(above)* and keeps a red-cheeked salamander comfortably moist in a tuft of moss as she records data *(below and right)*.

Red-cheeked salamanders need cool, moist mountain habitat.

Amy has collected tail tips from hundreds of red-cheeked salamanders within Great Smoky Mountains National Park. She takes the vials back to her lab to process them. "I take a little piece of the tail tissue and mash it up, heat it to break up all the cells and release the DNA," Amy explains. Each DNA sample ends up as a clear liquid in a little tube. Amy processes the DNA to isolate, copy, and clean up the genes she's interested in. "Then I send it off to be sequenced," she says. A genetics lab runs each salamander DNA sample through a machine that decodes it into a sequence of chemical building blocks.

Decoding Differences

Decoded DNA is complicated stuff. Each decoded salamander DNA sequence is a string of letters with more than a thousand combinations. Amy uses a computer program to help compare the DNA sequences. It measures the genetic differences among the hundreds of salamanders and helps arrange them into a family tree. "It tells you how each individual is related to each other individual," Amy explains. Each branch of the family tree is composed of the salamanders most closely related to one another.

What does the family tree show? The DNA of red-cheeked salamanders isn't the same throughout the park. The hundreds of individual salamanders Amy has tested fall into three different but related groups. Each group, or lineage, has unique ancestors. This means that the ancestors of each of those three salamander lineages were separated long enough for them to become different from one another during their generations apart. "We can see evidence of that past history retained in their genes today," says Amy. Even more interesting is what happens when you combine the red-cheeked salamander family tree with a map of the park (see map on p. 59). The members of the three salamander lineages cluster together into three separate park regions: the same three sections that had pockets of suitable climate twenty thousand years ago. The genetic information tells the same story as the past climate model.

What is that story, exactly? When the climate changed and was colder twenty thousand years ago, some red-cheeked salamanders lived in different parts of the park than they do now. Those too far up the mountain were frozen out, while those living at lower elevations were okay. Cooler temperatures created areas of unsuitable habitat. These became impassable barriers between salamander populations, dividing them into three separate groups. After the glacial cycle ended and the climate rewarmed, members of those three groups spread out and repopulated newly suitable microclimates. That long-ago separation remains encoded in the salamanders' genes. "There's a signature of the past," says Amy.

58

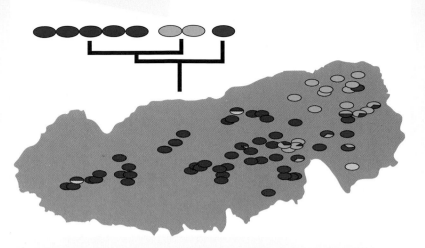

Each red-cheeked salamander whose DNA Amy collected is represented by a circle on the map that shows where it was found. The salamanders most genetically related to each other share one of three colors that correspond to the red, yellow, or blue lineages illustrated on the family tree (above map). The three lineages are different because their ancestors were separated into the only three regions of the park suitable for red-cheeked salamanders 20,000 years ago.

"I study population genetics," Amy Luxbacher says about the kind of science she does. "Basically, how different populations are related to one another; how they are distributed in an area; what their geographic range is; and if populations that live close by one another are more closely related to each other than they are to populations that, for example, live across a mountain from each other."

Planning for the Future

What does all this mean for today's red-cheeked salamanders? The climate change happening now is not a slow, natural glacial cycle. The current warming of Earth is caused by people and pollution and is happening very fast. Are there lessons from the past that could help us plan for the future?

Absolutely, Amy says. Thanks to her research, we know what happened to red-cheeked salamanders when the climate changed in the past. The salamanders that were living where conditions became unsuitable died out. They did not adapt to the cold twenty thousand years ago. Nor did they pack up and move. They simply survived in pockets of suitable habitats near their current homes. "Red-cheeked salamanders belong to a very old

Red-cheeked salamanders are terrestrial amphibians, living their entire life on land.

family," says Amy. "And have always occurred in cool, moist microclimates similar to where these guys are today." They're not built to handle extreme cold, and definitely not warmer and drier conditions. The only salamanders that survived where those that already lived where their needed microclimate remained.

How red-cheeked salamanders responded to climate change in the past is most likely how they will respond in the future, says Amy. They can't migrate or adapt. "They're going to need to stay where the conditions are suitable." Where exactly will that be? The same climate model that predicted past and present salamander habitat in the park has also created a map predicting where red-cheeked salamanders will likely live in the future (see "3° C Warmer Future" map on p. 54). The bad news is that the future map shows that a 5–6°F (3°C) rise in our planet's temperature will radically change the climate of the Smoky Mountains. That much warming will erase about two-thirds of current red-cheeked salamander habitat.

What's the good news? A third of red-cheeked salamander habitat seems likely to stick around. The future map shows that a few areas of good salamander microclimate will remain. Some red-cheeked salamander populations may survive on the highest moist mountaintops. Another refuge could be the park's coves. Coves are small Appalachian Mountain valleys with at least one closed-off end. "Cool, wet conditions sort of stay in the sheltered coves," explains Amy. "Those are still predicted to stay suitable, which might be a really good thing for these salamanders." Especially compared with extinction.

No matter what the future brings, Amy hopes that her research will help park managers better protect salamanders like the red-cheeked from climate change. "They're very concerned about preserving species in the park and trying to figure out how to protect them," says Amy. Knowing that red-cheeked salamanders in three different areas of the park are genetically different is an important piece of that puzzle. "As a national park, they want to try to maintain their biodiversity," says Amy. To do that, Great Smoky Mountains National Park will have to make sure that at least some members of all three salamander lineages survive. Amy will be sure to let them know what her salamander searches turn up.

Chapter 6

A Living Light Show

Summer sunsets at Great Smoky Mountains National Park signal the start of a living light show of fireflies.

There's something special about being in the woods at night. Doubly so when those woods are deep in the hills of Great Smoky Mountains National Park. The darkness is filled with sounds: water tumbling down a nearby stony creek, crickets and katydids, and leaves shuffling under the feet of small, scurrying creatures. A trio of hikers chat in whispers as they amble along an abandoned road that's now a walking trail. With no streetlights, cars, or houses around, it's definitely "country dark." Their steps are lit only with dim flashlight beams. Those too are extinguished once the three night hikers take

The firefly scientist Lynn Faust and her entomologist colleague Larry Buschman surrounded by the light show.

The only lights now are a few flashes between shadowy tree trunks. There are dim yellow blinking lights and some impossibly bright pops of white light. Every once in a while a very faint moving greenish blue glow appears. This hazy light doesn't flash. Instead it floats about a foot or so above the ground in an up-and-down ripple. The blue light is so dim, it's hard to know if it's real. Are your eyes playing tricks? "Nope, it's there," says a petite woman named Lynn Faust. "Those are called blue ghosts." The eerie blue ghosts and all the other glowing things are kinds of fireflies, or lightning bugs. "You can call them either thing," says Lynn with a cheery Tennessee twang. She should know. Lynn Faust is an expert on fireflies of the Appalachians, and a scientist who studies them.

"Won't be long now," says Lynn, checking the time. These lightning bugs are just a preview. Lynn and the other hikers are here for the main event—the light show that happens for a few weeks in June each year. Tonight it starts slowly, with patches of yellow blinking fireflies showing up in the forest. Then all of a sudden, they're everywhere. Hundreds of fireflies blink all at the same time and in perfect unison! Like a string of flashing holiday lights, they flash on-off-on-off all together about six times. Then, as if someone pulled the plug, they stop flashing for a number of seconds. With what seems like the flip of a switch, the fireflies start up again, repeating their perfectly timed display in a flawless harmony of flashes, then darkness, then flashes. It feels unreal, like some kind of enchanted dreamland. "You're surrounded by the fireflies," describes Lynn. "It's awe inspiring, it's rhythmic, and it's bright."

Who are the star performers in this amazing light show? A small, slender beetle called *Photinus carolinus*, the synchronous firefly of the Appalachians. It's one of only a handful of firefly species in the entire world known to flash as a group in synchrony. They can be found from North Georgia to Pennsylvania, says Lynn. "But they are in the highest densities here in the Smoky Mountains." Their summer display near Elkmont, Tennessee, has become the most famous in North America. "It's magical, beautiful, and remains a mystery even to the scientists," she says. In fact, scientists didn't even know about the phenomenon until recently.

New to Science

Lynn Faust grew up spending summers in the Smokies. Her family had a cabin in Elkmont, an old logging town turned vacation village that's now part of Great Smoky Mountains

Fireflies, like this synchronous firefly (*Photinus carolinus*), are a kind of beetle.

National Park. Like most kids, she loved to chase and catch fireflies and put them in jars to glow like lanterns. Her family and neighbors delighted in the annual arrival of the synchronous fireflies. "We'd wrap ourselves in blankets at night and sit on our porch and watch the light show," recalls Lynn. "We didn't realize nobody knew they were there," she recalls. Not until she read an article in a 1991 science magazine.

The magazine's feature story was about how a particular kind of Southeast Asian firefly uniquely flashes in unison. The article seemed to say, recalls Lynn, "that there were no real synchronous fireflies in the United States." She set out to make sure someone did know about them. After getting a phone call from Lynn, the firefly biologist Jonathan Copeland visited Elkmont in the summer of 1993. To his amazement, it was true. North America had synchronous fireflies! What Lynn Faust and other locals had taken for granted all their lives was a new discovery to science. Go figure!

Beetles That Glow

As new discoveries often do, identifying the synchronous fireflies brought a flood of questions from scientists. Why are they just in the Appalachian region? How and why do they sync their flashing? Are they closely related to other lightning bugs? Fireflies come in about two thousand species worldwide. These insects are a kind of beetle—the most diverse group of animals on the planet. "One of every five living creatures on Earth is a beetle," says Lynn. Like all beetles, fireflies are insects with wings with hard coverings (think ladybug). They hatch from eggs into grub like larvae, then metamorphose into pupae before again changing into flying adults.

What makes fireflies special is their bioluminescence, or living light. Firefly light shines from an organ, called a lantern, on the bottom of the abdomen. Specialized cells in the lantern produce light-emitting substances that glow when mixed with oxygen from chemical reactions. All fireflies flash or glow in

The light organ, or lantern, of a firefly is on its abdomen.

one or more of their life stages. Depending on the species, a firefly's lantern may glow during its long larva or pupa life stages as well. Fireflies live underground as larvae, hunting and eating worms and other creatures for a year or longer. Once they pupate and emerge as adults, winged flying fireflies often live just long enough to reproduce. Finding a mate is what the bright flashing of flying adults is all about. The kind, color, and pattern of flashes identify a firefly to a potential mate and announce where it is. It's a kind of courtship language, communicated in light.

The synchronous fireflies of the Smokies have their own unique light dance. It takes place only during a couple of weeks each summer after the adults have emerged. Well after sunset, when the forest is completely dark, is when synchronous fireflies search for mates. "You'll mainly see the males flashing," explains Lynn. "The females are mostly hidden down in the leaf litter." The light show's stage has females on the ground in the open spaces between trees with the males flying up above

them. The males begin, simultaneously blinking a series of six or so quick flashes over about three seconds: FLASH-FLASH-FLASH-FLASH-FLASH-FLASH. Then the males pause their flashing for around six seconds, each one waiting in darkness for his signal to be answered. "That's when the female flashes. She'll flash halfway through that roughly six seconds," says Lynn. The female flash is different. It's not synchronized with other females on the ground. Each female just counters with two quick, dim "I'm here" flashes: FLASH-FLASH. When the males see it, they scramble to go find her. Seeing a female flash in response is quite a sight, says Lynn. "The males start dropping out of the sky to get to her." Meanwhile, those males unlucky in love start their silent call again: FLASH-FLASH-FLASH-FLASH-FLASH-FLASH, wait-in-darkness, FLASH-FLASH-FLASH-FLASH-FLASH-FLASH, wait-in-darkness . . . "The adults live only a few weeks," says Lynn. "Their entire mission is to find a mate, lay eggs, and ensure that the next generation will have the light show next year."

64

A Firefly's Life Is Full of Change

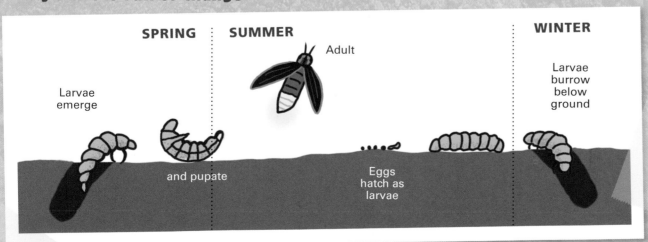

SPRING | SUMMER | WINTER

Larvae emerge

and pupate

Adult

Eggs hatch as larvae

Larvae burrow below ground

It's the male synchronous fireflies
that fly and flash among the trees.
Females respond with flashes from
the leaf litter below.

The How and Why

It took Lynn and other scientists a couple of summers to decipher the code of the male synchronous fireflies. "What these guys do is pretty complex—six flashes, and six seconds of dark, then six flashes," says Lynn. Sensitive video cameras connected to computers helped the scientists precisely measure the half second between each flash by males. The series of six flashes usually takes about three seconds, at least when air

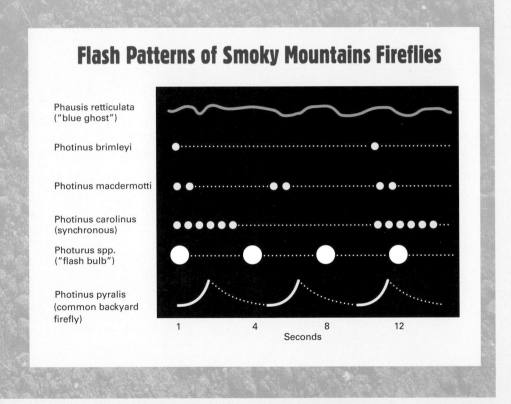

Flash Patterns of Smoky Mountains Fireflies

Phausis retticulata ("blue ghost")

Photinus brimleyi

Photinus macdermotti

Photinus carolinus (synchronous)

Photurus spp. ("flash bulb")

Photinus pyralis (common backyard firefly)

1   4   8   12
Seconds

temperatures are about average. Warmer nights make for faster flashing, and if temperatures drop below 53°F (12°C), all flashing stops.

Once the flashing pattern was figured out, the next

question was *How?*. How are the males able to sync their flashing? To find out, researchers set up some simple lab experiments. They placed two male synchronous fireflies side by side but divided by a barrier so they couldn't see each other. Each male firefly flashed alone to his own rhythm. When the barrier was removed, the two males synced up their flashing. It's all about whom they can see, explains Lynn. "They synchronize with their nearest neighbors." This makes sense if you think about the female firefly's perspective during the light show. She's down on the ground, so she only sees the males directly above her. Only viewable males need to perform and try to get her attention. That leads to the really big question—the mystery of *why*. Why does this one Smoky Mountains species of firefly flash in unison?

Male fireflies are competing to mate with females. What advantage does synchrony give them when finding a mate? No one knows for sure, but scientists have some ideas. Maybe the brighter combined light makes the males visible to females in a wider area. Or perhaps it's a way to help females identify the males as their own species—because they're singing in unison instead of all signaling "I'm for you!" separately. Another possibility is that neighbor males join in the flashing to try to steal mates from those already courting with back-and-forth signals. Why exactly they synchronize is still unclear, as are many things about these popular insects. "The bright firefly world is actually very murky," says Lynn.

Firefly Central

The door takes a strong tug to open. It finally gives way with a breezy whoosh. Apparently airlocks aren't just for spaceships. This one leads into a white room filled floor to ceiling with

above and right: **Becky Nichols, a park entomologist, and Lynn Faust** *(wearing hat)* **look through the firefly specimens in the collections room.**

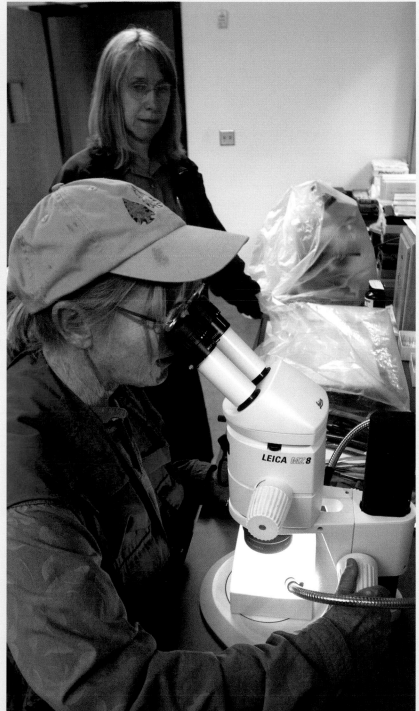

white cabinets and drawers. The air-sealed room is the museum collections room at Great Smoky Mountains National Park's Science Center. A uniformed park entomologist named Becky Nichols hovers over an opened drawer next to Lynn Faust. Inside are dozens and dozens of local firefly specimens. Each insect is pinned down, with a tiny label attached. Lynn looks closely at the insects, trying to find a rare firefly species she has yet to see in the wild. Identifying fireflies is not easy, as many look incredibly alike. "The southestern U.S. with its mountains, valleys, and coastal plains is one of the richest regions in the

Lynn Faust is studying many kinds of fireflies in the Appalachians, including some that don't light up. *Ellychnia* fireflies hang out on tree trunks like this one, are active during the day, and have no lanterns.

world for fireflies, with at least fifty different species," says Lynn.

Why are the Smokies so suited to lightning bugs? Moist mature forest is the key. All that thick, damp, rotting leaf litter is full of firefly larvae food. Fireflies like the synchronous also need forests of older large trees with little underbrush. Mating fireflies would have a hard time finding each other in

Data loggers, like the one Lynn is using above, record temperatures at the ground level, where fireflies emerge as adults in late spring.

thickets and bushes. "We have more than twenty species here in this area alone. And each one of the species is equally interesting and mysterious," says Lynn. "Some of the fireflies have lanterns and beautiful light shows, and others have lost their lanterns through evolution and have other ways of communicating." There are fireflies with yellow lights, orange flickering lights, white flashbulb lights, blue floating, glowing lights—and ones that don't light up at all. Some fireflies, like the synchronous, don't eat at all as adults, while others are voracious predators that hunt other insects, including other fireflies. Predator fireflies are the ones with the bright white popping and greenish flashes.

Fireflies flash to find mates, but lighting up also attracts hungry hunters. Predators know about the light show too. Fireflies taste bad, so most birds, bats, and frogs avoid them. Fireflies that hunt other fireflies aren't bothered by the bad taste, and even seek out the worst-tasting predator fireflies to boost their own chemical defenses. There are also predator fireflies that lure in prey by imitating the flash of other species.

If that's not tricky enough, there are a whole bunch of firefly mimic insects. They look like bad-tasting fireflies, but are really moths, crickets, beetles, or some other bug. "Everybody's fooling everybody," says Lynn. Figuring out who's doing what to whom and why is part of the fun of firefly research. "I am constantly humbled and amazed by all the clever adaptations, survival strategies, and

By collecting information on daily temperatures in the park, Lynn Faust can predict when synchronous fireflies will emerge and begin flashing. This helps park managers plan for the crowds that come to see the light show every summer.

intricate relationships of these seemingly simple beetles who glow or flash." Lynn's been studying fireflies for more than twenty years now. "I kind of fell into this accidentally," she says. After bringing the synchronous fireflies to the attention of scientists, she became involved in their study too. "And those fireflies took me into the whole world of fireflies." Projects involving all sorts of lightning bugs keep her busy these days.

Loved, but Not Always Protected

Firefly research helps fireflies, too. Firefly populations around the world are in decline. It can be difficult to protect them without understanding their entire life cycle. A good example is a synchronous Southeast Asian firefly that flash in unison from trees along a river. When their numbers began plummeting, people protected the trees—but it didn't help. The fireflies continued to disappear. "Finally somebody asked, 'Where do the larvae live?' And no one knew," says Lynn. It turns out that the larvae depend on nearby habitat that's quickly being turned into farmland—not the protected trees. "How can you conserve something if you don't know anything about its life history?" asks Lynn.

Fireflies spend most of their lives as soil-living larvae, so they are vulnerable to poisoning from pesticides and herbicides. A chemically treated, lush, weed-free green lawn is not good for firefly larvae. Plowing up, bulldozing under, or paving over soil kills them as well. The females of some firefly species can't fly, so are unable to escape or migrate if their habitat is destroyed. Another threat to adult fireflies is light pollution from homes and businesses

Lynn finds fireflies endlessly fascinating. "Fireflies are one of the few insects people are not trying to kill."

near mating fireflies. Lynn has seen firsthand how blue ghost firefly populations have been erased due to the floodlights of newly built homes. "There's so much light that the males can't find the females or vice versa," explains Lynn. It's why the park is so important to fireflies. It's a place without habitat destruction, light pollution, or farm and lawn pesticides. "These

Synchronous fireflies know exactly when to start flashing each night. "It's as though they wear little watches," says Lynn Faust.

are lucky little fireflies that live in the Smokies," says Lynn. "They don't have the challenges that most fireflies worldwide have outside of parks."

The park visitors who see the amazing light show of the synchronous fireflies are lucky too. "The fireflies gather by the thousands on peak nights," says Lynn. "And people

gather by the thousands on peak nights to see them in Great Smoky Mountains National Park." Families with little kids, old folks with walkers, Scout groups, and people of all kinds start arriving toward dusk. Like a fireworks display crowd, they bring chairs or blankets to sit on and patiently wait for nightfall. When darkness finally arrives, everyone stays put,

and most speak in whispers. Being in the woods at night is something special, after all. Soon enough the fireflies begin their courtship. They call and respond to each other in a language of perfectly timed flashes of light created by their own bodies. "It's got nothing to do with humans," says Lynn. "Yet we get to witness one of nature's finest shows."

People enjoying nature's best in one of America's protected, treasured places. It's what the national parks are all about.

Lynn points out a few of the twenty or so different kinds of fireflies that live in the Smokies, such as the Photinus carolinus above.

Words to Know

Appalachians–an eastern North American mountain range that stretches 1,500 miles (2,400 km) from the Canadian province of Quebec to central Alabama.

biodiversity–the variety of species of animals and plants in an environment.

biologist–a scientist who studies living things.

bioluminescence–the light produced and given off by living organisms, such as fireflies and jellyfish.

caldera–a large, deep, bowl-shaped crater formed by a volcanic explosion.

citizen science–scientific research done by nonscientists.

DNA–deoxyribonucleic acid; the substance in genes that passes on the characteristics of living organisms.

ecologist–a scientist who studies the relationships between living things and their environment.

ecosystem–a system made up of a group of living things, its environment, and the relationships between them.

endangered–in danger of becoming extinct.

Endangered Species Act–A U.S. federal law passed in 1973 that protects endangered and threatened wildlife and plants from hunting, collecting, and harm to them or their habitats.

geologist–a scientist who studies Earth's crust of rock.

geothermal–heat from within the Earth.

geyser–a hot spring that shoots out hot water and steam.

geyserite–deposited silica that forms around hot springs.

glacial cycle–a period of cooler worldwide temperatures that expands ice sheets and glaciers; an ice age or glacial age.

global climate change–the rise in the average temperature of Earth's atmosphere and oceans since the late nineteenth century; global warming.

GPS–a device that uses Global Positioning System signals from a network of satellite links to pinpoint locations.

habitat–the place where an animal or plant naturally lives.

herpetologist–a scientist who studies amphibians and/or reptiles.

hydrothermal–high-temperature water conditions near Earth's surface.

lantern–the light-producing organ of a firefly.

larva–an immature form of an animal that undergoes metamorphosis.

magma–melted, liquid rock under the ground.

metamorphosis–the process of changing from an immature to an adult stage in some animals, including insects and amphibians.

microchip–a miniature electronic circuit.

microclimate–the climate of a very small, specific area.

migrate–to move from one region to another when conditions change.

mimic–an animal evolved to look like another for benefit or protection.

model–a computer simulation based on mathematical equations and entered data.

native–plants and animals that evolved in a place and were not brought in from someplace else; indigenous.

nocturnal–active at night.

nonnative–plants and animals brought in from another place; exotic.

omnivore–an animal that eats both animal and plant foods.

osteoderm–a bony plate in the skin of some reptiles.

population–a group of organisms of the same species living in the same place.

scat–animal droppings or poop.

species–a category of living things made up of related individuals able to produce offspring that can themselves reproduce.

telemetry–a technology for remote measurement, tracking, and reporting of information.

terrestrial–living on the land, not in water.

threatened–not currently endangered but still threatened with extinction or likely to be endangered in the near future.

venom–a toxic substance in animals that is actively delivered to a targeted victim.

Quote Sources & Selected Bibliography by Chapter

1. Natural Wonders of Water and Heat

All quotes from the Yellowstone National Park geologists Henry (Hank) Heasler and Cheryl Jaworowski are from voice-recorded interviews with the scientists on May 2, 2012 onsite at the park, except the following:

"Yellowstone is truly a magical place…" Shoemaker, Jennifer. *Yellowstone's Restless Giant.* National Park Service online video. 2007. www.nps.gov/yell/photosmultimedia/yellowstone-indepth-episode-1.htm

"If that were the case…" Hottle, Dan. May 19, 2011. Yellowstone National Park News Feature: *Iconic Yellowstone Boardwalks More Than "Old West" Attraction.*

"So rather than build…" Ibid.

Brantley, Steven R., Jacob B. Lowenstern, Robert L. Christiansen, Robert B. Smith, Henry Heasler, Greg Waite, and Charles Wicks. "Tracking Changes in Yellowstone's Restless Volcanic System." USGS Fact Sheet 100-03, p 1. 2004. pubs.usgs.gov/fs/fs100-03

Lowenstern, Jacob B., Robert L. Christiansen, Robert B. Smith, Lisa A. Morgan, and Henry Heasler. "Steam Explosions, Earthquakes, and Volcanic Eruptions—What's in Yellowstone's Future?" USGS Fact Sheet 2005-3024. 2005. pubs.usgs.gov/fs/2005/3024

2. Yellowstone's Biggest Bears

All quotes from the wildlife biologist Mark Haroldson are from voice-recorded interviews made on April 30, 2012, onsite at his USGS: Northern Rocky Mountain Science Center office in Bozeman, Montana, and were reviewed by the scientist. Quotes from the Yellowstone National Park Ranger Dave Page are from an in-person interview of May 5, 2012, onsite at Yellowstone National Park.

Interagency Grizzly Bear Study Team. US Geological Survey website: nrmsc.usgs.gov/research/igbst

Leatherman, D. A., I. Aguayo, and T. M. Mehall* (9/11) "Mountain Pine Beetle." Colorado State University Fact Sheet: Mountain Pine Beetle. www.ext.colostate.edu/pubs/insect/05528.html

Marris, Emma. "The End of the Wild." *Nature* 469, no. 7329 (Jan. 13, 2011): 150–52.

Schwartz, C. C., M. A. Haroldson, and K. A. Gunther. "Understanding Grizzlies: Science of the Interagency Grizzly Bear Study Team," in *Knowing Yellowstone: Science in America's First National Park.* Edited by J. Johnson. Lanham, Md.: Taylor Trade Publishing, 2010.

3. Tracking Monsters

All quotes from the University of Arizona herpetologist Kevin Bonine are from voice-recorded interviews made on October 24, 2011, in Tucson, Arizona, and were reviewed by the scientist. Brian Park quotes are from voice-recorded interviews made on October 22, 2011, in Saguaro National Park and October 24, 2011, in Tucson, Arizona, and were reviewed by him as well.

Beck, Daniel D. *Biology of Gila Monsters and Beaded Lizards.* Berkeley: University of California Press, 2005.

Goth, Brenna. "Gila Monsters Getting DNA Swab Treatment." Arizona Daily Star, Oct. 14, 2012.

4. Counting Cacti

Quotes from Tucson, Arizona, AmeriSchools College Prep Academy students Arron Davis, Alex Varela, and Almomese Ramirez are from onsite interviews at Saguaro National Park during BioBlitz on October 21, 2011. All quotes from the Saguaro National Park biologist Don Swann are from voice-recorded interview during BioBlitz on October 21, 2011, or a telephone interview of November 3, 2012, and were reviewed by him.

Kreutz, Doug. "Older Saguaros Are Still Paying a Price After Great Freeze of 2011." *McLatchy-Tribune Business News*, Jan. 12, 2012.

Swann, Don E., Adam C. Springer, and Kara O'Brien. "Using Citizen Science to Study Saguaros and Climate Change at Saguaro National Park." *ParkScience* 28, no. 1 (2011): 69–72. www.nature.nps.gov/ParkScience/index.cfm?ArticleID=486

5. Smoky Mountain Salamanders

Quotes from the evolutionary ecologist Amy Luxbacher are from voice-recorded interviews either onsite at Great Smoky Mountains National Park on September 17, 2012, or a telephone interview with her on December 12, 2012, and all were reviewed by her.

Hoffman, Keith. *Climate Change and the Red-Cheeked Salamander.* National Park Service video: www.nps.gov/grsm/photosmultimedia/climate-video1.htm.

Milanovich J. R., W. E. Peterman, N. P. Nibbelink, and J. C. Maerz. "Projected Loss of a Salamander Diversity Hotspot as a Consequence of Projected Global Climate Change." PLoS ONE 5, no. 8 (2010).

Ruben, J. A., and A. J. Boucot. "The Origin of the Lungless Salamanders (Amphibia: Plethodontidae)." *American Naturalist* 134 (1989): 161–69.

6. A Living Light Show

Quotes from the researcher Lynn Faust are from voice-recorded interviews onsite at Great Smoky Mountains National Park on May 14–15, 2012, and were reviewed by her.

Brown, Robbie. "Fireflies, Following Their Leader, Become a Tourist Beacon." *New York Times*, June 15, 2011.

Milius, Susan. "US Fireflies Flashing in Unison: A Rare, Dazzling Spectacle May Not Be Limited to Far-Flung Places." *Science News* 155, no. 11 (March 13, 1999): 168.

Yellowstone park staff post signs near trails to alert visitors of bear sightings.

WARNING
05/01/2012
Near Cache Cr. Ford

BEAR FREQUENTING AREA

Removal of this sign may result in INJURY to others and is punishable by law

THERE IS NO GUARANTEE OF YOUR SAFETY WHILE HIKING OR CAMPING IN BEAR COUNTRY

Index

Page numbers in **bold** type refer to photos and their captions.

SCIENTISTS IN THE FIELD
Where Science Meets Adventure

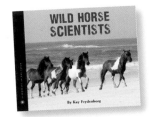

Check out these titles to meet more scientists who are out in the field—and contributing every day to our knowledge of the world around us:

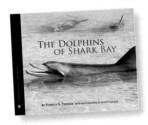

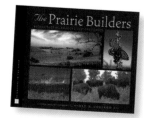

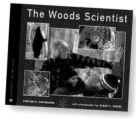

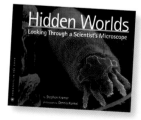

Looking for even more adventure? Craving updates on the work of your favorite scientists, as well as in-depth video footage, audio, photography, and more? Then visit the new Scientists in the Field website!

www.sciencemeetsadventure.com